Lakshmi Puran: The Bestower of Fortune

(English Edition)

Featuring Original Oriya Verses with English Transliteration and Translation

UNMESHA JENA

Title: Lakshmi Puran- The Bestower of Fortune (English Edition)

Author: Unmesha Jena

ISBN: 978-93-343-6536-8

First Edition: 2025

Preface

The *Lakshmi Puran* holds a sacred place in the hearts of devotees across the Indian subcontinent and beyond. Rooted in the ancient traditions of Sanatana Dharma, this revered text narrates the compassionate grace of Goddess Lakshmi, the embodiment of wealth, purity, and righteousness. It is more than a religious scripture—it is a spiritual guide that emphasizes devotion, equality, and ethical living.

Composed originally in Oriya, the *Lakshmi Puran* is traditionally recited on Thursdays in the month of Margasira (November–December), particularly by women who observe *Manabasa Gurubar*. This observance celebrates the Goddess's visit to the homes of those who maintain cleanliness, devotion, and humility—regardless of social status. The Purana also conveys powerful messages against discrimination and affirms the dignity of all beings, including marginalized communities. Through its verses, it promotes the idea that true devotion lies in purity of heart and action, not in caste, class, or ritual alone.

This book is a humble effort to transliterate the original Oriya text and render it in English, so that the profound wisdom of the *Lakshmi Puran* can reach a wider audience. The transliteration retains the lyrical beauty of the original, while the translation seeks to convey its meaning with clarity and reverence. It is intended not only for readers familiar with Oriya but also for the younger generation and global readers who wish to connect with this timeless tradition.

With gratitude to the divine light within and around us,
Unmesha Jena
Translator
Lakshmi Puran – English Edition

The Author

The author is an experienced IT Project Manager with a deep-rooted spiritual inclination. Driven by personal devotion to Goddess Lakshmi and inspired by Her generous heart, she has undertaken the task of translating sacred texts to make their timeless teachings more accessible to today's readers.

This is her second book, following the successful publication of her first work titled *Surya Puran: The Radiance of Dharma (English Edition)*, which is also meant for readers seeking spiritual depth and cultural insight.

She graduated with a Bachelor of Technology degree in 2015, securing the top rank in the Computer Science department. Alongside her professional and academic pursuits, she had been a Classical Odissi dancer for more than 12 years—an experience that reflects her long-standing appreciation for Indian culture, art, and literature.

The purpose behind this translation is to share the compassionate grace, moral strength, and transformative blessings of Goddess Lakshmi with a wider audience, transcending linguistic boundaries. Through this work, the author hopes to illuminate the values of humility, devotion, and equality as exemplified in the *Lakshmi Puran*, and to inspire readers to invite the Goddess's presence into their lives—not just as the bestower of material wealth, but as the embodiment of purity, generosity, and inner prosperity.

Acknowledgement

With heartfelt devotion and humility, I offer my deepest gratitude to Goddess Lakshmi, whose boundless grace, compassion, and divine presence have inspired this work. It is Her sacred blessings that gave me the inner strength and clarity to undertake the transliteration and translation of the *Lakshmi Puran*. May Her light continue to illuminate the hearts of all who seek wisdom, purity, and prosperity.

I am profoundly thankful to my family—for their unwavering support, encouragement, and patience throughout this journey. Their faith in the spiritual and cultural significance of this work has been a constant source of motivation and strength.

I also extend my sincere appreciation to every reader and devotee, whose reverence for tradition and openness to understanding has given this book its true purpose. May these pages bring you closer to the divine virtues of humility, devotion, and righteousness.

A special homage goes to Mahakavi Balarama Dasa, the great 16th-century Oriya poet and saint, whose original composition of the *Lakshmi Puran* continues to inspire generations. His vision, courage, and literary brilliance made it possible to preserve a scripture that transcends time, challenging social norms while upholding eternal values.

This work is dedicated to all who walk the path of truth and devotion.

Table of Contents

CHAPTER 1

THE LAKSHMI PURAN

ମାଣବସା ଲକ୍ଷ୍ମୀ ପୁରାଣ

Māṇabasā Lakṣmī Purāṇa

The Purana of Lakshmi related to Māṇabasā observance

Sri Mahalakshmi Ashtakam

ନମୋସ୍ତୁ ତେ ମହାମାୟେ ଶ୍ରୀପୀଠେ ସୁର ପୂଜିତେ ।

ଶଙ୍ଖ ଚକ୍ର ଗଦା ହସ୍ତେ ମହାଲକ୍ଷ୍ମୀ ନମୋସ୍ତୁ ତେ ।୧।

Namos tu te mahāmāye śrīpīṭhe sura pūjite

Śaṅkha cakra gadā haste mahālakṣmī namo's tu te

Salutations to you, O Great Enchantress (Mahāmāyā), who resides in the seat of prosperity (Śrīpīṭha), and is worshipped by the gods.

O Mahalakshmi, who holds the conch, discus, and mace in her hands — salutations to you.

ନମସ୍ତେ ଗରୁଡ଼ାରୁଢ଼େ କୋଲାସୁର ଭୟଙ୍କରୀ ।

ସର୍ବ ପାପ ହରେ ଦେବି ମହାଲକ୍ଷ୍ମୀ ନମୋସ୍ତୁ ତେ ॥

Namaste garuḍārūḍhe koḷāsura bhayaṅkarī

Sarva pāpa hare devi mahālakṣmī namo's tu te

Salutations to you who rides Garuda and is terrifying to the demon Kolasura.

O Goddess who destroys all sins — O Mahalakshmi, salutations to you.

ସର୍ବଜ୍ଞେ ସର୍ବାବରଦେ ସର୍ବ ଦୁଷ୍ଟ ଭୟଙ୍କରୀ ।

ସର୍ବ ଦୁଃଖ ହରେ ଦେବି ମହାଲକ୍ଷ୍ମୀ ନମୋସ୍ତୁ ତେ ।୩।

Sarvajñe sarvāvarade sarva duṣṭa bhayaṅkarī

Sarva duḥkha hare devi mahālakṣmī namo's tu te

O All-knowing one, Granter of all boons, Terrifier of all evil beings —

O Goddess who removes all sorrows — O Mahalakshmi, salutations to you.

ସିଦ୍ଧି ବୁଦ୍ଧି ପ୍ରଦେ ଦେବି ଭୁକ୍ତି ମୁକ୍ତି ପ୍ରଦାୟିନୀ।

ମନ୍ତ୍ରମୂର୍ତ୍ତେ ସଦା ଦେବି ମହାଲକ୍ଷ୍ମୀ । ନମୋସ୍ତୁ ତେ ।୪।

Siddhi buddhi prade devi bhukti mukti pradāyinī

Mantramūrtbhe sadā devi mahālakṣmī namo's tu te

O Goddess who grants accomplishments and wisdom, and bestows both enjoyment and liberation —

You are the embodiment of mantra — O Goddess Mahalakshmi, salutations to you.

ଅଦ୍ୟନ୍ତ ରହିତେ ଦେବି ଆଦ୍ୟାଶକ୍ତି ମାହେଶ୍ୱରୀ ।

ଯୋଗେନ ଯୋଗସମ୍ଭୁତେ ମହାଲକ୍ଷ୍ମୀ ନମୋସ୍ତୁ ତେ ।୫।

Adyanta rahite devi ādyāśakti māheśvarī

Yogena yogasambhute mahālakṣmī namo's tu te

O infinite one, without beginning or end, the primordial power, consort of Maheshwara (Shiva) —

Born of yoga and known through yoga — O Mahalakshmi, salutations to you.

ସ୍ଥୁଳସୂକ୍ଷ୍ମ ମହାରୌଦ୍ରେ ମହାଶକ୍ତି ମହୋଦରେ ।

ମହାପାପ ହରେ ଦେବି ମହାଲକ୍ଷ୍ମୀ ନମୋସ୍ତୁ ତେ । ୬ ।

Sthūlasūkṣma mahāraudre mahāśakti mahodare

Mahāpāpa hare devi mahālakṣmī namo's tu te

Gross and subtle, terribly fierce, Great Power, and of great belly (symbolic of capacity) —

O Goddess who destroys great sins — Mahalakshmi, salutations to you.

ପଦ୍ମାସନା ସ୍ଥିତେ ଦେବି ପରଂ ବ୍ରହ୍ମ ସ୍ୱରୂପିଣୀ ।

ମରମେଷ୍ଟି ଜଗନ୍ମାତ ମହାଲକ୍ଷ୍ମୀ ନମୋସ୍ତୁ ତେ ।୭।

Padmāsanā sthite devi paraṁ brahma svarūpiṇī

Marameṣṭi jaganmāta mahālakṣmī namo's tu te

Seated on a lotus, O Goddess, the very embodiment of the Supreme Brahman —

Beloved one, Mother of the universe — O Mahalakshmi, salutations to you.

ଶ୍ୱେତାମ୍ବର ଧରେ ଦେବି ନାନାଲଙ୍କାର ଭୂଷିତେ । ୭

ଜଗତ୍‌ସ୍ଥିତେ ମହାମାୟେ ମହାଲକ୍ଷ୍ମୀ ନମୋସ୍ତୁ ତେ ।୮।

Śvetāmbara dhare devi nānālaṅkāra bhūṣite

Jagatsthite mahāmāye mahālakṣmī namo's tu te

O Goddess clothed in white, adorned with many ornaments —

O Mahāmāyā who pervades the world — O Mahalakshmi, salutations to you.

ମହାଲକ୍ଷ୍ମୀ ଷ୍ଟକଂ ଯଃ ପଠତେ ଭକ୍ତିମାନ୍ନରଃ ।

ସର୍ବ ସିଦ୍ଧି ମବାପ୍ନୋତି ରାଜଂ ପ୍ରାପ୍ନୋତି ସର୍ବଦା ।୯।

Mahālakṣmīṣṭakaṁ yaḥ paṭhate bhaktimān naraḥ

Sarva siddhi mavāpnoti rājaṁ prāpnoti sarvadā

Whoever recites this Mahalakshmi Ashtakam with devotion —

Attains all accomplishments and gains royal status always.

ଏକ କାଳଂ ପଠେନ୍ନିତ୍ୟଂ ମହାପାପ ବିନାଶନଂ ।

ଦ୍ୱିକାଳଂ ଯଃ ପଠେନ୍ନିତ୍ୟଂ ଧନଧାନ୍ୟ ସମନ୍ୱିତଃ ।୧୦।

Eka kālaṁ paṭhen nityaṁ mahāpāpa vināśanam

Dvikālaṁ yaḥ paṭhen nityaṁ dhanadhānya samanvitaḥ

Reading it once a day destroys great sins.

Reading it twice daily grants wealth and grain (prosperity).

ତ୍ରିକାଳଂ ଯଃ ପଠେନ୍ନିତ୍ୟଂ ମହାଶତ୍ରୁ ବିନାଶକ ।

ମହାଲକ୍ଷ୍ମୀ ଭବେନ୍ନିତ୍ୟଂ ପ୍ରସନ ବରଦା ଶୁଭ ।୧୧।

Trikālaṁ yaḥ paṭhen nityaṁ mahāśatru vināśakaḥ

Mahālakṣmī bhaven nityaṁ prasanna varadā śubha

He who recites it thrice daily destroys even great enemies.

Mahalakshmi remains ever pleased and grants boons and auspiciousness.

ଇତି ଶ୍ରୀଇନ୍ଦ୍ର କୃତଂ ଶ୍ରୀ ମହାଲକ୍ଷ୍ମୀଙ୍କ ଅଷ୍ଟକଂ ସମ୍ପୂର୍ଣ୍ଣମ୍ ।

Iti śrī indra kṛtaṁ śrī mahālakṣmīṅka aṣṭakaṁ sampūrṇam

Thus ends the Mahalakshmi Ashtakam composed by Shri Indra.

Lakshmi Puran Begins

ନମସ୍ତେ କମଳା ମାଗୋ ସାଗର ଦୁଲଣୀ । ନମସ୍ତେ ନମସ୍ତେ ଲକ୍ଷ୍ମୀ ବିଷ୍ଣୁଙ୍କ ଘରଣୀ ॥

Namaste Kamalā māgo sāmara dulaṇī I Namaste namaste lakṣmī Vishnuṅka gharaṇī II

Salutations to you, O Kamala (Lakshmi), dear Mother, the beloved of Samara (Lord Vishnu). | Salutations, salutations to Lakshmi, consort of Vishnu.

ନମସ୍ତେ କମଳାଳୟା ଅତି ଦୟାବତୀ । ସ୍ଥାବର ଜଙ୍ଗମ କୀଟ ଆଦି ପାଳୁ ନିତି ॥

Namaste Kamalāḷayā ati dayāvatī I Sthāvara jaṅgama kīṭādi pāḷu niti II

Salutations to the one who dwells in the lotus, very compassionate. | You constantly protect all—from immobile beings to moving ones, insects, and others.

ତୋର ଦୟାବଳେ ମାଗୋ ଦରିଦ୍ର ଜନର । ହୁଅଇ ଅଚଳ ବିତ୍ତ ଜିଣଇ କୁବେର ॥

Tora dayābaḷe mago daridra janara I Huāi acala vitta jiṇaī kubera II

By your compassion, O Mother, the poor person... | ...becomes firmly wealthy, surpassing even Kubera.

ତୋର ଦ୍ରୋହୀଜନେ ମାଗୋ ଅନ୍ନ ନ ମିଳଇ | ଯେତେ ଅରଜିଲେ କେବେ ପେଟ ନ ପୁରଇ ॥

Tora drohījane māgo anna na miḷāi I Jete Arajile kebe peṭa na puraī II

But your betrayer, O Mother, doesn't even get food... | No matter how much he begs, his hunger is never fulfilled.

ତୋହର ଚରିତ ମନ ଦେଇ ଯେ ଶୁଣିଇ | କିଅବା ଭକତି ଭାବେ ସର୍ବଦା ଗୁଣଇ ॥

Tohara carita mana dei je śuṇī I Kiābā bhakti bhābe sarvadā guṇī II

Whoever attentively listens to your deeds... | Or praises your qualities with devotion always...

ତାହାର ଦରିଦ୍ରପଣ ଯାଏ ଦୂର ହୋଇ । ସର୍ବଦା ତାକୁ ପ୍ରସନ୍ନ ହେଉ ମହାମାୟୀ ॥

Tāhāra daridrapaṇa jāe dūra hoī I Sarvadā tāku prasanna heu mahāmāyī II

His poverty goes far away... | And Mahamaya (the Great Enchantress) is always pleased with him.

ଏଣୁ ତୋ ଚରଣେ ମାଗୋ ଅଶେଷ ପ୍ରଣାମ । କରୁଛି ପୁରାଅ ବାରେ ମୋର ମନସ୍କାମ ॥

Eṇu to caraṇe māgo aśeṣa praṇāma I Karuchi purāa bāre mora manaskāma II

Therefore, at your feet, O Mother, countless salutations... | I offer, please fulfil all my heartfelt desires.

ତୋ ଚରିତ କିଞ୍ଚିତେ ମୁଁ କରିବି ରଚନ । ଜଗତ ଜନନୀ ବାରେ ଦିଅ ଦିବ୍ୟଜ୍ଞାନ ॥

To carita kiñcite muñ karibi racanā I Jagata jananī bāre dia divyajñāna II

Let me compose a little about your deeds... | O Mother of the Universe, bestow me divine knowledge.

ଦିନେକ ନାରଦ ପରାଶର ମୁନି ଦୁଇ । ଭ୍ରମି ଭ୍ରମି ଏକ ଗ୍ରାମେ ପ୍ରବେଶିଲେ ଯାଇ ॥

Dineka nārada parāśara muni dui I Bhrami bhrami eka grāme prabeśile jāi II

One day, sages Nārada and Parāśara—both sages— | Wandering and wandering, entered a certain village.

ସେହିଦିନ ମାର୍ଗଶୀର ମାସ ଗୁରୁବାର । ପର୍ବ ପଡ଼ିଥିଲା ସର୍ବ ପୁରବାସୀଙ୍କର ॥

Sehi dina mārgaśīra māsa gurubāra I Parba paḍithilā sarba purabāsīṅkara II

That day was a Thursday in the month of Mārgaśīra (a sacred lunar month). | A festival of the local residents was being observed.

ପ୍ରତି ଘରଦ୍ୱାର ଗୋମୟରେ ଲିପା ହୋଇ । ଲକ୍ଷ୍ମୀ ପାଦପଦ୍ମ ଚିତା ପଡ଼ିଥିଲା ତହିଁ ॥

Prati gharadvāra gomayare lipā hoī I Lakṣmī pādapadma citā paḍithilā tahiṅ II

Each doorstep was smeared with cow dung (a sacred purifying act). | The footprints of Lakshmi were drawn (depicted) there.

ନାରୀମାନେ ସ୍ନାନସାରି ପିନ୍ଧି ଝୀନବାସ । ଲକ୍ଷ୍ମୀଙ୍କ ପୂଜାରେ ସର୍ବେ ହୋଇଛନ୍ତି ରତ ॥

Nārīmāne snānasāri piṅdhi jhīnabāsa I Lakṣmīnka pūjāre sarve haichanti rata II

The women, after bathing, wore clean and fine garments. | All were engrossed in the worship of Goddess Lakshmi.

ବ୍ରାହ୍ମଣଙ୍କଠାରୁ ଯେ ଚଣ୍ଡାଳ ପରିଯନ୍ତେ । ଲକ୍ଷ୍ମୀଙ୍କ ପୂଜାରେ ରତ ଅଛନ୍ତି ସମସ୍ତେ ॥

Brāhmaṇaṅkaṭhāru je caṇḍāḷa parijante I Lakṣmīnka pūjāre rata achanti samaste II

From the Brāhmaṇas to even the Chaṇḍālas (the lowest castes), | Everyone was engaged in the worship of Lakshmi.

ହୁଳହୁଳି ଶବଦରେ ପୂରିଛି ଗଗନ । ଦେଖି ଏ ଉତ୍ସବରୀତ ବିଧାତା ନନ୍ଦନ ॥

Huḷahuḷi śabda re purichi gagana I Dekhi e utsabarīta vidhātā nandana II

The sky was filled with sounds of hula-huli (joyful ululation). | Seeing this festive scene, the son of Brahmā (Nārada) rejoiced.

ପଚାରନ୍ତି ପରାଶର ମୁନିଙ୍କୁ ଉଦନ୍ତ । କହ କହ ତପୀବର ଏ କିସ ଚରିତ ॥

Pachāranti parāśara, muninku udanta I Kaha kaha tapīvara e kisa carita II

Parāśara asked, speaking to the sage (Nārada), | "Tell, tell, O great ascetic, what is this event?"

ବ୍ରାହ୍ମଣୁ ଚଣ୍ଡାଳ ଆଦି ସମସ୍ତ ଜାତିରେ । କରୁଛନ୍ତି କି ଉତ୍ସବ ଆନନ୍ଦ ମତିରେ ॥

Brāhmaṇu caṇḍāḷādi samasta jātire I Karuchanti ki utsava ānanda matire II

From Brāhmaṇas to Chaṇḍālas and others, all castes— | Why are they all celebrating joyfully in their hearts?

କେଉଁ ବ୍ରତ କି ଭପାସ ଅଟେ ଏହାନାମ | କାହାକୁ କରନ୍ତି ପୂଜା ତାର କି ନିୟମ ॥

Keuṅ brata ki bhapāsa aṭe ehānāma I Kāhāku karanti pūjā, tāra ki niyama II

What is the name of this vrata (vow) or ritual that is being observed? | To whom is the worship being offered, and what are its rules?

ଏହା ଶୁଣି ପରାଶର ହୋଇ ହସ ହସ | କହନ୍ତି ବଚନ ଧୀରେ ଶୁଣ ବିଧିଶିଷ ॥

Ehā śuṇi parāśara hoī hasa hasa I Kahanti bacana dhīre, śuṇa vidhisiṣa II

Hearing this, Parāśara gently smiled. | He said calmly, "Listen, O best of knowers of dharma (divine law)."

ଏ ଧନମାଣିକା ଗୁରୁବାର ଯେ ଅଟଇ । ଲକ୍ଷ୍ମୀ ଦେବୀଙ୍କର ପୂଜା ଏ ବ୍ରତେ ଘଟଇ ॥

E dhanamāṇikā gurubāra je aṭai I Lakṣmī devīṅkara pūjā e brate ghaṭai II

This is the sacred "Dhanamaṇikā" Thursday that is being observed. | It is in this vrata (vow/ritual) that the worship of Goddess Lakshmi is performed.

ସବୁମାସ ମାନଙ୍କରେ ମାର୍ଗଶୀର ସାର | ତହିଁରେ ପଡ଼ଇ ଯେଉଁ ଯେଉଁ ଗୁରୁବାର ॥

Sabumāsa mānankare mārgaśīra sāra I Tahiṅre paḍai jeuṅ jeuṅ gurubāra II

Among all the months, Mārgaśīra is the essence (most auspicious). | Whichever Thursdays fall in it (Mārgaśīra),

ଲକ୍ଷ୍ମୀଙ୍କର ପ୍ରିୟ ସେହି ବାରମାନ ଜାଣ | ସବୁଠାରୁ ଆଦ୍ୟ ଗୁରୁବାର ଯେ ପ୍ରଧାନ ॥

Lakṣmīnkara priya sehi bāramāna jāṇa I Sabuṭhāru ādya gurubāra je pradhāna II

Know those days as dear to Lakshmi. | Among them, the first Thursday is the foremost (most important).

ଏକ ଦିନେ ଶୁକ୍ଳଦଶମୀ ଗୁରୁବାର । ପଡ଼ିଲେ ସୁଦଶାବ୍ରତ ହୁଏ ସେ ଦିନର ॥

Eka dine śukḷadaśamī gurubāra । Paḍile sudasābrata hue se dinara ॥

If a Thursday falls on the tenth day of the waxing moon (Śukla Daśamī), | Then that day is observed as the Sudashā-vrata.

ଲକ୍ଷ୍ମୀଙ୍କର ଅତିପ୍ରିୟ ଅଟଇ ସେ ବ୍ରତ । ଏହାକହି ପରାଶର ହେଲେ ମୌନବ୍ରତ ॥

Lakṣmīnkara atipriya aṭai se brata । Ehākahi parāśara hele maunabrata ॥

That vrata is extremely dear to Goddess Lakshmi. | Saying this, Parāśara became silent (entered a vow of silence).

ପୁଣି ତାହାଙ୍କୁ ପୁଚ୍ଛିଲେ ବ୍ରହ୍ମାଙ୍କ କୁମର । ଲକ୍ଷ୍ମୀବ୍ରତ କରିଥିଲେ ମର୍ତ୍ତ୍ୟେ କେଉଁ ନର ॥

Puṇi tāhāṅku puchchhile brahmāṅka kumāra । Lakṣmībrata karithile martye keuṅ nara ॥

Then Brahmā's son (Nārada) asked him again: | Which human (man) had observed the Lakshmi-vrata while on Earth?

ତହିଁରେ ସେ କେଉଁ ଶୁଭ ଫଳ ଲଭିଅଛି | ଲକ୍ଷ୍ମୀ ଦ୍ରୋହୀ ହୋଇକରି କେ ଦୁଃଖ ପାଇଛି ॥

Tahiṅre se keuṅ śubha phala labhi achi । Lakṣmī drohī hoīkari ke duḥkha pāichi ॥

Who among them has received that auspicious result? | And who has suffered by turning against Lakshmi (being a betrayer of Lakshmi)?

ଏହା ସବୁ ମୋ ଆଗରେ କହତ ଗୋସାଇଁ | ଶୁଣିବାକୁ ତାହା ଚିତ୍ତେ ଶ୍ରଦ୍ଧା ଉପୁଜଇ ॥

Ehā sabu mo āgare kahata <u>gosāīn</u> । Śuṇibāku tāhā citte śraddhā upujai ॥

O revered one, please tell all this in front of me. | Just by hearing it, my ears will be filled with reverence.

ନାରଦ ବଚନ ଶୁଣି ପରାଶର ମୁନି । କହନ୍ତି ହରଷ ଚିତ୍ତେ ସୁମଧୁର ବାଣୀ ॥

Nārada bacana śuṇi parāśara muni । Kahanti haraṣa citte sumadhura vāṇī ॥

Hearing the words of Nārada, the sage Parāśara | Spoke with a joyful heart and sweet speech.

ଧନ୍ୟ ହେ ନାରଦ ତୁମ୍ଭେ ପବିତ୍ର ଚରିତ୍ର । ଲକ୍ଷ୍ମୀବ୍ରତ କଥାରେ ଯେ ହୋଇଅଛ ରତ ॥

Dhaṇya he nārada tum̐bhe pavitra caritra I Lakṣmībrata kathāre je hoiacha rata II

Blessed are you, Nārada, of pure character, | Who have become devoted to the story of Lakshmi-vrata.

କହୁଅଛି ପୁରାତନ କଥା ଅଛି ଯାହା | ହୋଇବ ଆନନ୍ଦ ଜାତ ଶୁଣିଲେଟି ତାହା ॥

Kahuachhi purātana kathā achhi jāhā I Hoiba ānanda jāta śuṇileṭi tāhā II

I will now tell an ancient story that exists, | Hearing which, joy will naturally arise.

ଏକଦିନେ ଜଗନ୍ନାଥ ପାଶେ ଲକ୍ଷ୍ମୀ ଥିଲେ | କରପତ୍ର ଯୋଡ଼ିଣ ତାହାଙ୍କୁ ଜଣାଇଲେ ॥

Ekadine Jagannātha pāśe Lakṣmī thile I Karapatra joḍiṇa tāhāṅku jaṇāile II

One day, Lakshmi was with Lord Jagannath. | With joined palms, she informed Him.

ଆଜି ମୋ ବାରର ବ୍ରତ ପଡ଼ିଲା ଗୋସାଇଁ । ତୁମ୍ଭେ ଆଜ୍ଞାଦେଲେ ନଗ୍ର ବୁଲିଯିବି ମୁହିଁ ॥

Āji mo bārara brata paḍilā gosāiṅ I Tumbhe ājñādele nagra bulijibi muhiṅ II

Today is the day of my weekly vow, O Lord. | If you permit, I shall go around the city.

ଗୋବିନ୍ଦ ବୋଇଲେ ଲକ୍ଷ୍ମୀ ନଗ୍ରହିଁ ବୁଲିବ । ଦଶମୀ ପାଳନା ଅନ୍ନ ବେଗେ ରାନ୍ଧିଦେବ ॥

Govinda bolile Lakṣmī nagrahiṅ buliba I Daśamī pāḷanā anna bege rāndhidebā II

Govinda (Jagannath) said, "Lakshmi, you may roam the city." | But on the Dashami (10th lunar day), cook the food early.

ପ୍ରଭୁଙ୍କ ମୁଖରୁ ମାତ ଏମନ୍ତ ଶୁଣିଲେ । ବସ୍ତ୍ର ଅଳଙ୍କାରମାନ ଯତନେ ପିନ୍ଧିଲେ ॥

Prabhuṅka mukharu māta emanta śuṇile I Bastra alaṅkāramāna jatane pindhile II

Hearing these words from the Lord's mouth, | She carefully wore her fine clothes and ornaments.

ନାସିକାରେ ନବରତ୍ନ ବସଣି ଖଞ୍ଜିଲେ । ଚଉସ୍ତରୀ ରତ୍ନମାଳା କଣ୍ଠେ ଲମ୍ବାଇଲେ ॥

Nāsikāre navaratna basaṇi khañjile I Causaṭarī ratnamālā kaṇṭhe lambāile II

She inserted a nine-gem nose ring in her nose. | She hung a four-tiered gem necklace around her neck.

କରରେ କାହୁଟି ରମ୍ୟବଳୟ କଙ୍କଣ । ସୁନା ସୁତା ମାଣିକ୍ୟ ପଦକ ଆଭରଣ ॥

Karare kāhuṭi ramyabaḷaya kaṅkaṇa I Sunā sutā māṇikya padaka ābharaṇa II

On her hands were beautiful bangles and bracelets of gold. | Golden chains and ruby pendants adorned her neck.

ବାଜେଣି ନୂପୁର ମାତା ପଦରେ ଖଞ୍ଜିଲେ | ଏପରି ନାନା ଭୂଷଣେ ସୁବେଶ ହୋଇଲେ ॥

Bājeṇi nūpura mātā padare khañjile I Epari nānā bhūṣaṇe subeśa hoile II

She placed anklets with jingling bells on her feet. | Thus adorned with various ornaments, she appeared splendid.

ଯେବଣ ମାତାଙ୍କ ଅଧିକାର ତିନିପୁର | ଆଭରଣ କେତେ ମାତ୍ର ଦେବି ପଟ୍ଟାନ୍ତର ॥

Jebaṇa mātāṅka adhikāra tinipura । Ābharaṇa kete mātra debi paṭṭāntara ॥

She who has dominion over the three worlds, | How many ornaments can one describe of the Goddess?

ଶୁଣ ହେ ନାରଦ ଏହା ହୋଇ ଏକଚିତ୍ତ । ବୃଦ୍ଧା ବ୍ରାହ୍ମଣୀ ରୂପକୁ ଧରି ଜଗନ୍ନାଥ ॥

Śuṇa he Nārada ehā hoi ekacitta । Vṛuddhā brāhmaṇī rūpaku dhari Jagannātha ॥

Listen, O Narada, being of one focused mind, | Lord Jagannath assumed the form of an old Brahmin woman.

ପବେଶ ହୋଇଲେ ଯାଇଁ ସାଧୁର ଦୁଆରେ । ସାଧବାଣୀ ଉଭା ହୋଇଥିଲେ ସେହିଠାରେ ॥

Prabeśa hoile jāi sādhura du'āra । Sādhavāṇī ubhā hoithile sehiṭhāre ॥

He entered and went to the house of a noble lady. | The noble woman was standing there at that spot.

ତାକୁ ଦେଖି ମହାଲକ୍ଷ୍ମୀ କହନ୍ତି ବଚନ । ଶୁଣ ଶୁଣ ସାଧବାଣୀ ହୋଇ ସ୍ଥିରମନ ॥

Tāku dekhi Mahālakṣmī kahanti bacana I Śuṇa śuṇa sādhavāṇī hoi sthiramana II

Seeing her, Mahalakshmi spoke these words: | "Listen, O noble woman, with a steady mind."

ଆଜିପରା ମହାଲକ୍ଷ୍ମୀ ବ୍ରତ ଗୁରୁବାର । ଲିପା ପୋଛା କରିନାହୁଁ କିମ୍ପା ଘରଦ୍ୱାର ॥

Ājiparā Mahālakṣmī brata gurubāra I Lipā pochā karināhuṅ kimpā gharadvāra II

From today begins the Mahalakshmi fast on Thursday. | Have you not plastered or cleaned the house and doorway yet?

ସାଧବାଣୀ ଏହା ଶୁଣି ବୋଲଇ ସେ କ୍ଷଣି । କି ରୂପେ ଏ ବ୍ରତ ହୁଏ କାହା ପୂଜାପୁଣି ॥

Sādhavāṇī ehā śuṇi bolai se kṣaṇi I Ki rūpe e brata hue, kāhā pūjāpuṇi? II

Hearing this, the noble lady (housewife) instantly spoke: | In what manner is this fast observed, and who is worshipped?

ବୁଝାଇ ତା ସବୁ କହ ହେ ନାନୀଗୋସାଇଁ | ଅଇଲେ ମନକୁ ମୁଁ ଏ ବ୍ରତ କରିବଇଁ ॥

Bujhāi tā sabu kaha he nānīgosāiṅ I Aile manaku muṅ e brata karibaiṅ II

Explain everything to me, O old mother! | If my heart agrees, I shall observe this fast.

ଏହାଶୁଣି ପଦ୍ମାଳୟା କହନ୍ତି ସଧୀରେ । ଶୁଣ ସାଧବାଣୀ ବ୍ରତ ହୁଏ ଏ ବିଧିରେ ॥

Ehāśuṇi Padmāḷayā kahanti sadhīre I Śuṇa sādhavāṇī brata hue e vidhire II

Hearing this, Padmalaya (Goddess Lakshmi) spoke gently: | Listen, O noble lady, this fast is performed in this way:

ମାର୍ଗଶୀର ମାସେ ଯେଉଁ ଆଦ୍ୟ ଗୁରୁବାର | ସେଦିନ ଉଷାରୁ ଶେଯ ଛାଡ଼ି ତତପର ॥

Mārgaśīra māse jeuṅ ādhya gurubāra I Sedina uṣāru śeṣa chāḍi tatpara II

On the first Thursday of the month of Margashira, | One must be attentive from early morning till the end of the day.

ଗୋମୟ ଜଳରେ ଘର ଦୁଆର ଲିପିବ । ଲକ୍ଷ୍ମୀଦେବୀ ପାଦପଦ୍ମ ଚିତାକୁ ଲେଖିବ ॥

Gomaya jalare ghara du'āra lipiba I Lakṣmīdevī pādapadma citāku lekhība II

The house and doorway are to be plastered with cow dung and water. | The footprint design of Goddess Lakshmi is to be drawn.

ନୂଆ ମାଣ ଗୋଟିଏ ଅଣାଇ ଯତ୍ନେ ବେଗେ । ଧୋଇ ଧାଇ କରି ତାକୁ ଶୁଖାଇବ ବେଗେ ॥

Nūā māṇa goṭie aṇāi jatne bege I Dhoi dhāi kari tāku śukhāiba bege II

Bring a new measuring pot (rice measure) carefully and promptly. | Wash and clean it, and dry it quickly.

ତାହାକୁ କରିବ ନାନା ଚିତ୍ର ଯେ ବିଚିତ୍ର । ଚାଉଳକୁ ବାଟି ଚିତା ଲେଖିବ ସମସ୍ତ ॥

Tāhāku kariba nānā citra je vicitra I Cāuḷaku bāṭi citā lekhība samasta II

That (surface or space) will be decorated with various strange (beautiful) drawings. | Everyone will grind rice and draw sacred patterns (designs) with it.

ତହିଁ ସ୍ନାନ କରିଆସି ହୋଇ ରୁଚିମନ୍ତ । ଚଉକି ବା ଖଟୁଲିଏ ଆଣିବ ତ୍ୱରିତ ॥

Tahiṅ snāna kari āsi hoi rucimanta I Cauki bā khaṭuliye āṇiba tvarita II

Thereafter, one must bathe and return, becoming pure-minded (devoted). | A wooden seat or stool is to be brought quickly.

ତାକୁ ଧୋଇ ତାରପରେ ଦେବ ନୂଆଧାନ । ରଙ୍ଗକଳା ନୋହି ହୋଇଥିବ ଶୁକ୍ଳବର୍ଣ୍ଣ ॥

Tāku dhoi tārapare deba nūādhāna I Raṅgakalā nohi hoithiba śuklabaṛṇa II

It will be washed, and fresh paddy (unhusked rice) will be placed on it. | It should not be colored but should be white in appearance.

ତହୁଁ କିଛି କୁଢ଼ାଇ ଯେ ସେ ନୂଆମାଣରେ | ଧାନମାଣ ଯେ ପୁରାଇ ରଖିବ ତା ପରେ ॥

Tahuṅ kichhi kuḍhāi je se nūāmāṇare I Dhānamāṇa je purāi rakhība tā pare II

Then a little of that will be shifted into a new measuring pot. | The measure will be filled completely with paddy and kept thereafter.

ସେ ଧାନ ମାଣ ଉପରେ ଗୁଆ ତିନିଗୋଟି । ହଳଦୀ ପାଣିରେ ତାହା ଧୋଇ ଥୋଇବଟି ॥

Se dhāna māṇa upare guā tinigoṭi I Haḷadī pāṇire tāhā dhoi thoibāṭi II

Three betel nuts will be placed on top of that paddy pot. | They will be washed in turmeric water and placed there.

ଶୁକଳ ଧାନର ଶିଖା ରଖି ବେଣ୍ଟିକରି । ମାଣ ଉପରେ ତାହାକୁ ଥୋଇବ ବିଚାରି ॥

Śukla dhānara śikhā rakhi beṇṭi kari I Māṇa upare tāhāku thoiba bicāri II

A tuft of white paddy will be tied (like a knot or braid). | That will be thoughtfully placed atop the paddy measure.

ଚୁଳ ଆଖୁ ମୂଳା କଦଳୀରେ ସଜାଡ଼ିବ । ପଟ୍ଟାଦି ରଙ୍ଗବସନ ପୁଷ୍ପେ ମଣ୍ଡାଇବ ॥

Cuḷa ākhu mūḷā kadaḷīre sajāḍiba I Paṭṭādi raṅgavasana puṣpe maṇḍāiba II

The hearth, sugarcane, radish, and banana plant will be arranged decoratively. | With silk and colorful clothes, along with flowers, it will be adorned.

ତହୁଁ ଆବାହନ ମହାଲକ୍ଷ୍ମୀଙ୍କୁ କରିବ । ଗନ୍ଧପୁଷ୍ପ ଧୂପଦୀପ ଆଦି ସମର୍ପିବ ॥

Tahuṅ ābāhana Mahālakṣmīṅku kariba I Gandhapuṣpa dhūpadīpa ādi samarpiba II

Then Goddess Mahalakshmi will be invoked (invitation ritual performed). | Fragrance, flowers, incense, lamps, etc., will be offered.

ପ୍ରଥମରେ ବାଳଧୂପ ତାପରେ ଶଙ୍କୁଡ଼ି । ଏପରି କରିବ ତିନିଧୂପକୁ ସଜାଡ଼ି ॥

Prathamare bāḷadhūpa tāpare śaṅkuḍi I Epari kariba tinidhūpaku sajāḍi II

First comes the offering of mild incense, then conch (ritual blowing or lamp). | In this way, three incense offerings will be arranged.

ମହାଲକ୍ଷ୍ମୀଙ୍କର ଆଉ ଏକ ବ୍ରତ ଅଛି । ସୁଦଶା ବୋଲି ତା ନାମ ଲୋକେ ପ୍ରକଟିଛି ॥

Mahālakṣmīṅkara āu eka brata achi I Sudaśā boli tā nāma loke prakaṭichi II

There is another vow (vrata) of Goddess Mahalakshmi. | Its name is Sudasha, as it is known among the people.

ଶୁକଳଦଶମୀ ହେଲେ ଗୁରୁବାର ଦିନ । ହୁଅଇ ସୁଦଶାବ୍ରତ ଶୁଣ ଦେଇ ମନ ॥

Śukḷadaśamī hele gurubāra dina I Huai sudaśābrata śuṇa dei mana II

When the bright tenth day (Shukla Dashami) falls on a Thursday, | That day is observed as Sudasha Vrata—listen with attention.

ସେହିଦିନ ଉଷାରୁ ଯେ ଉଠି ତତପର । ଝୋଟି ଆଦି ଚିତା ଦେବ ପୂର୍ବ ପରକାର ॥

Sehi dina uṣāru je uṭhi tatpara I Jhoṭi ādi citā deba pūrba parakāra II

On that day, rising from dawn, one should be devoted (active). | Designs like jhoti (alpona) should be drawn as per earlier tradition.

ସ୍ନାନ ସାରି ଗୃହେ ପଦ୍ମମଣ୍ଡଳ ଲେଖିବ । ତହିଁପରେ ଧୋଇ ଏକ ଖଟୁଲି ରଖିବ ॥

Snāna sāri gṛuhe padmamaṇḍala lekhiba I Tahiṅpare dhoi eka khaṭuli rakhība II

After bathing, one should draw the lotus-circle (lotus motif) in the house. | Then a small wooden stool (khatuli) should be washed and placed there.

ତହିଁପରେ ଲକ୍ଷ୍ମୀପୂଜା ଗୁଆକୁ ଥୋଇବ । ପଞ୍ଚାମୃତ ଶୁଦ୍ଧଜଳେ ସ୍ନାନ କରାଇବ ॥

Tahiṅpare lakṣmīpūjā guāku thoība I Pañcāmṛta śuddhajale snāna karāiba II

After that, in Lakshmi's worship, a betel nut (symbolic offering) will be placed. | It (the offering or idol) will be bathed with Panchamrita and pure water.

ଦଶଖିଅ ସୂତାରେ ଯେ ବ୍ରତେକ କରିବ । ଲକ୍ଷ୍ମୀଙ୍କ ନାମରେ ଦଶଗୋଟି ଗଣ୍ଠି ଦେବ ॥

Daśakhi'a sūtāre je brateka kariba I Lakṣmīnka nāmare daśagoṭi ganṭhi deba II

With a ten-knotted thread, one will perform the vow (vrata). | In the name of Lakshmi, ten knots will be tied.

ଦଶକେରା ଦୁବରେ ଯେ ବ୍ରତ ଗୁଡ଼ାଇବ । ମହାଲକ୍ଷ୍ମୀ ଗୁଆ ପାଖେ ତାହାକୁ ଥୋଇବ ॥

Daśakerā dubare je brata guḍāiba I Mahālakṣmī guā pākhe tāhāku thoība II

With ten-bladed durva grass, the vrata (vow) will be wrapped/performed. | That (item) will be placed beside Mahalakshmi's betel nut offering.

କରୁଥିଲେ ପୂର୍ବରୁ ସେ ବ୍ରତ ପୁରାତନ । ବ୍ରତଡ଼ୋର ଆଣିତହିଁ ଥୋଇବ ବହନ ॥

Karuthile pūrburu se brata purātana I Bratadora āṇitahiṅ thoība bahana II

If the vow was done earlier, and is an old one, | Then the old sacred thread (vrata thread) will also be brought and placed there.

ପଥମରେ ବାଳଧୂପ ନଇବେଦ୍ୟ କରି | ତାପରେ ଯା ଭୋଗଦେବ ଶୁଣ ହେତୁକରି ॥

Pathamare bāḷadhūpa naibedya kari I Tāpare jā bhogadeba śuṇa hetukari II

First, a young incense (initial dhupa) will be offered as naivedya (offering). | After that, the main food offering will be made—listen to how it is done.

ଅରୁଆ ଚାଉଳ ଏକମାଣ ତିନ୍ତାଇବ । ତାକୁ କୁଟି ଚୂନା କରି ଯତନେ ରଖିବ ॥

Aruā cāuḷa ekamāṇa tintāiba I Tāku kuṭi cūnā kari jatane rakhība II

One measure of uncooked rice will be washed three times. | It will be ground into fine powder and carefully kept aside.

କଦଳୀ ନଡ଼ିଆ ଛେନା ଆଦି ଦଶପୁର । ଦେଇ ଦଶଗୋଟି ମଣ୍ଡା କରିବ ସତ୍ୱର ॥

Kadaḷī naḍiā chēnā ādi daśapura I Dei daśagoṭi maṇḍā kariba satvara II

Banana, coconut, chhena (cheese), etc.—ten types of ingredients (are used). | Using them, ten balls of rice cakes (maṇḍā) are quickly prepared.

ମହାଲକ୍ଷ୍ମୀଙ୍କୁ ତା ପୂଜାକରି ଭକ୍ତି ଚିତ୍ତେ । ସେ ପ୍ରସାଦ ଖାଇ ଦିନ ବଞ୍ଚିବ ଯେ ସୁସ୍ଥେ ॥

Mahālakṣmīṅku tā pūjā kari bhakti citte I Se prasāda khāi dina bañciba je susthe II

Worshipping Mahalakshmi with those, in a mind full of devotion, | By eating that prasad, the day will be lived in well-being.

ମହାଲକ୍ଷ୍ମୀ ପ୍ରସାଦ ଯେ ପରକୁ ନ ଦେବ | ବିଭା ହୋଇଥିବା ଝିଅ ସୁଦ୍ଧା ନ ଖାଇବ ॥

Mahālakṣmī prasāda je paraku na deba I Bibhā hoithibā jhi'a śuddhā na khāiba II

The prasad of Mahalakshmi should not be given to outsiders. | Even a married daughter, though pure, should not eat it.

ଯେ ଉତ୍ତାରୁ କଥା ଏକ ମନଦେଇ ଶୁଣ । ଗୁରୁବାର ଦିନ ଯେଉଁ କଥା ନିବାରଣ ॥

Je uttāru kathā eka manadei śuṇa । Gurubāra dina jeuṅ kathā nibāraṇa ॥

Now attentively listen to one more (final) instruction. | Some things are forbidden on Thursday (Gurubara vrata day).

ସେ କଥା କହୁଛି ଏବେ ସାଧବାଣୀ ଶୁଣ । କେବେ ନ ଭାଜିବ ଖଇ ଗୁରୁବାର ଦିନ ॥

Se kathā kahuchi ebe sādhavāṇī śuṇa । Kebe na bhājiba khai gurubāra dina ॥

Now I will tell that—listen, O noble housewife. | Never fry puffed paddy (khaee) on the day of Gurubara.

ଯେଉଁ ନାରୀ ଗୁରୁବାର ଦିନରେ ଆମିଷ । ଭୁଞ୍ଜଇ ଲୋଭରେ କିବା ନ ପଖାଳେ କେଶ ॥

Jeuṅ nārī gurubāra dinare āmiṣa । Bhuñjai lobhare kibā na pakhāḷe keśā ॥

The woman who, on the day of Thursday (Gurubara), eats non vegetarian food out of greed, | Or do not cleanse the hair with water,

ଭୁଞ୍ଜଇ ଉଚ୍ଛିଷ୍ଟ କିବା ଲଗାଇ ଯେ ତେଲ । ମହାଲକ୍ଷ୍ମୀ ତାର ନିଶ୍ଚେ ଭାଙ୍ଗିବେଟି ଗେଲ ॥

Bhuñjai uccișța kibā lagāi je tela I Mahālakṣmī tāra niśce bhāṅkibeṭi gela II

Or eats someone's leftover food or applies oil, | Mahalakshmi will certainly break away from her (leave her) and go.

ଗୁରୁବାରେ ଯେଉଁ ନାରୀ ତୁଳାକୁ ଭିଣଇ । ଲାଉରେ ଆମିଷ ଦେଇ ଯେ ଗ୍ରାସ କରଇ ॥

Gurubāre jeuṅ nārī tuḷāku bhiṇai I Lā'ure āmiṣa dei je grāsa karai II

Any woman who even touches the weighing scale on a Thursday, | Or who eats food cooked in bottle gourd with meat (non-veg),

ଖଟର ଛାୟାରେ ଯେହୁ କରଇ ଶୟନ । ରାତ୍ରକାଳେ ଦଧିଅନ୍ନ ଯେ କରେ ଭୋଜନ ॥

Khaṭara chāyāre jehu karai śayana I Rātrakāle dadhianna je kare bhojana II

Who sleeps under the shadow of a cot, | Or who eats curd-rice during the night,

କ୍ଷୌର ହୁଏ ଯେହୁ ଯାଇ ନାପିତର ଦ୍ୱାରେ । ଭୋଜନ ସମୟେ ଅନ୍ନ ପକାଏ ଭୂମିରେ ॥

Kṣaura hue jehu jāi nāpitara dvāre I Bhojana samaye anna pakāe bhūmire II

Or who gets a haircut going to the barber's house (on Thursday), | Or who drops rice directly on the ground during mealtime,

ଭୁଞ୍ଜି ନ ପାରିଣ ଅନ୍ନ ଫୋପାଡ଼ିଣ ଦିଏ । ଏଡ଼େକର୍ମ ଯେ କରେ ସେ ଲକ୍ଷ୍ମୀଙ୍କୁ ନ ପାଏ ॥

Bhuñji na pāriṇa anna phopāḍiṇa die I Eḍekarma je kare se lakṣmīṅku na pāe II

She who cannot eat the food and throws it away carelessly, | One who commits such acts does not receive (the grace of) Goddess Lakshmi.

ଗୁରୁବାର ଦିନ ସକାଳରୁ ଗୋମୟରେ | ଦୁଆର ଯେ ନ ଲିପଇ ଅଳସ ପଣରେ ॥

Gurubāra dina sakāḷaru gomayare I Du'āra je na lipai alasa paṇare II

On Thursday morning, in cow dung water (used ritually), | If the doorstep is not smeared due to laziness,

ଚୁଲିରୁ ନ କାଢ଼େ ପାଂଶ ଭକ୍ଷେ ଯେ ଆମିଷ | ଏମାନଙ୍କଠାରେ ଲକ୍ଷ୍ମୀ କରନ୍ତି ଯେ ରୋଷ ॥

Cuḷiru na kāḍhe pāṅśa bhakṣe je āmiṣa I Emānankaṭhāre lakṣmī karanti je roṣa II

If she does not clean the ashes from the hearth and eats meat, | Towards such people, Goddess Lakshmi becomes angry.

ଧନ ଜନ ସବୁ ତାର ହରଣ କରନ୍ତି । ମାଗିଗଲେ ଅନ୍ନବସ୍ତ୍ର କେହି ନ ଦିଅନ୍ତି ॥

Dhana jana sabu tāra haraṇa karanti I Māgigale annavastra kehi na dianti II

All wealth and people (supporters) are taken away from her. | Even if she begs, no one gives her food or clothing.

ଗୁରୁବାରେ ଯେଉଁନାରୀ ପିନ୍ଧେ ଶୁକ୍ଳଲୁଗା । ଐଶ୍ୱର୍ଯ୍ୟ ସମ୍ପଦ ପାଏ ହୁଅଇ ସୁଭଗା ॥

Gurubāre jeuṅ nārī pindhe śuklalu'gā I Aiśvarya sampada pāe huai subhagā II

The woman who wears white clothes on Thursday, | She attains wealth and prosperity and becomes fortunate.

ଗୁରୁବାରେ ଯେଉଁ ନାରୀ ପିଲାଙ୍କୁ ମାରଇ । କିବା ପାକହାଣ୍ଡି ଧୋଇ କଳା ନ ଛାଡ଼ଇ ॥

Gurubāre jeuṅ nārī piḷāṅku mārai | Kibā pākahāṇḍi dhoi kaḷā na chāḍai ||

The woman who beats children on a Thursday, | Or even after washing a black cooking pot, its blackness doesn't go away,

ସନ୍ଧ୍ୟା ଗଡ଼ିଗଲେ ଯେ ଦିଅଇ ସନ୍ଧ୍ୟାବତୀ । ପୁତ୍ରଧନ ହାନି ହୁଏ ସଦା ହୁଏ ବହୁ କ୍ଷତି ॥

Sandhyā gaḍigale je di'ai sandhyāvatī | Putradhana hāni hue sadā hue bahu kṣati ||

She who lights the evening lamp only after dusk passes, | Suffers loss of sons and wealth, and constantly faces great misfortune.

ଗୁରୁବାରେ ଯେଉଁ ନାରୀ ପୋଡ଼ାଦ୍ରବ୍ୟ ଖାଏ । ଶୋଇବାର ଶଯ୍ୟା ବଙ୍କା କରିଣ ବିଛାଏ ॥

Gurubāre jeuṅ nārī poḍādrabya khāe | Śoibāra śajya baṅkā kariṇa bichāe ||

The woman who eats roasted or burnt food on Thursday, | And arranges her bed unevenly (untidily) for sleeping,

ଶାଶୁ ଶ୍ୱଶୁରଙ୍କୁ ନ ମାନଇ ଯେ ରମଣୀ । ଉଲଗ୍ନ ହୋଇ ଶୟନ କରଇ ଯେଉଁ ପ୍ରାଣୀ ॥

Śāśu śvaśuranku na mānai je ramaṇī | Ulagna hoi śayana karai jeun prāṇī ||

The woman who does not respect her mother-in-law and father-in-law, | Any being who sleeps unclothed,

ଅମାବାସ୍ୟା ସଂକ୍ରାନ୍ତିରେ ବୁଲାଏ ଯେ ହଳ ।ଏହି ଦିନମାନଙ୍କରେ ଘେନଇ ତଇଳ ॥

Amāvāsyā saṅkrāntire būlāe je haḷa | Ehi dinamāṅkare ghenai taila ||

Who ploughs the field (or engages in farming work) on Amavasya (new moon) or Sankranti (sun transition days), | And who uses oil for bathing or massage on these forbidden days,

ସଭାରେ ବସିଣ ଯେ ମାନବ ମିଛ କହି । ଆଳସ୍ୟେ ପାଦ ନ ଧୋଇ ଯେ ଭୁଞ୍ଜି ବସଇ ॥

Sabhāre basiṇa je mānaba micha kahi | Ālasye pāda na dhoi je bhuñji basai ||

The person who sits in an assembly and tells lies, | And eats food without washing feet out of laziness,

କୁଷ୍ମାଣ୍ଡ ଫଳକୁ ଯେହୁ ରମଣୀ କାଟଇ । ଋତୁମତୀ ନାରୀକି ଯେ ରମଣ କରଇ ॥

Kuṣmāṇḍa phalaku jehu ramaṇī kāṭai | Ratumatī nārīki je ramaṇa karai ॥

The woman who cuts the white gourd fruit (considered sacred or avoided at times), | Or a man who has intercourse with a menstruating woman,

କନ୍ୟା ତୁଳା ମାସେ ପିତୃଶ୍ରାଦ୍ଧ ନ କରଇ | କଥା କହୁ କହୁ ସବୁବେଳେ ଯେ ହସଇ ॥

Kanyā tuḷā māse pitṛuśrāddha na karai | Kathā kahu kahu sabubeḷe je hasai ॥

Who does not perform ancestral rituals (Shraddha) during the months of Kanya (Virgo) and Tula (Libra), | And who laughs all the time while speaking, in a frivolous or mocking way,

ଏମନ୍ତ ମନୁଷ୍ୟ ସଦା ବହୁକଷ୍ଟ ପାଇ । ଆୟବୁଦ୍ଧି ନାଶଯାଏ ଅନ୍ନ ନ ମିଳଇ ॥

Emanta manuṣya sadā bahukaṣṭa pāi | Āyabuddhi nāśajāe anna na miḷai ॥

Such a person always suffers great hardships. | Their income and intelligence are destroyed, and they don't get food.

ଗୁରୁବାର ସଙ୍କରାନ୍ତି ଅମାବାସ୍ୟା ଦିନ । ରଜନୀରେ ସ୍ତ୍ରୀ ପୁରୁଷ କଲେକ ଭୋଜନ ॥

Gurubāra saṅkarānti amāvāsyā dina | Rajanīre strī puruṣa kaleka bhojana ||

On Thursdays, Sankranti, and Amavasya (new moon) days, | If a man and woman dine together (especially at night),

କିବା ଏହି ତିନି ଦିନ ଯେଉଁ ନାରୀ ମୋହେ । ପୁରୁଷ ସଙ୍ଗରେ ମାତି ଧର୍ମକୁ ନ ଚାହେଁ ॥

Kibā ehi tini dina jeun nārī mohe | Puruṣa saṅgare māti dharmaku na cāhen ||

Or if a woman indulges in sensual acts on these three days, | Getting intimate with a man, ignoring religious conduct,

ପ୍ରାଣେ ନାଶ ନ କରିଣ ତାକୁ ଦୁଃଖ ଦେଇ । ବୁଲାନ୍ତି ଯେ ଅନ୍ନବସ୍ତ୍ର କାହିଁ ନ ମିଳଇ ॥

Prāṇe nāśa na kariṇa tāku duḥkha dei | Bulānti je annabhastra kāhĩn na miḷai ||

Even if she doesn't lose her life, she suffers deeply. | She wanders, but cannot obtain food or clothing.

ଏତିକି ଦିନରେ ଯେହୁ ତିକ୍ତଦ୍ରବ୍ୟ ଖାନ୍ତି । ଅନ୍ତଃକାଳେ ଯମଦ୍ୱାରେ ବହୁ ଦଣ୍ଡ ପାନ୍ତି ॥

Etiki dinare jehu tiktadravya khānti | Antaḥkāle jamadvāre bahu daṇḍa pānti ||

Those who consume bitter substances on these specific days, | At death, they receive severe punishment at Yama's (God of death) gate.

ଏ ତିନିଦିନ ଯେ ନାରୀ କରଇ ହବିଷ୍ୟ | ଦୁଃଖୀ ରଙ୍କି ଦେଖି ଦାନ କରଇ ବିଶେଷ ॥

E tinidina je nārī karai haviṣya | Duḥkhī raṅki dekhi dāna karai biśeṣa ||

A woman who performs sacred havishya (austere meal offerings) on these three days, | And seeing the poor and needy, gives in charity especially — (she earns special merit).

କରେ ଲକ୍ଷ୍ମୀବ୍ରତ ଲକ୍ଷ୍ମୀବାରେ ଉପବାସ । ବଢ଼ିବ ତାହାର ଧନ ଜନ ଆୟୁଯଶ ॥

Kare Lakṣmīvrata Lakṣmībāre upavāsa | Baḍhiba tāhāra dhana jana āyuyasha ||

One who observes Lakshmi Vrat and fasts on Lakshmi's day (Thursday), | Their wealth, family, lifespan, and fame shall increase.

ସକାଳୁ ଶେଯରୁ ଉଠି ଯେ ମୁଖ ନଧୁଏ । ତା ମୁଖ ଯେ ଜନ ଦେଖେ ତାର ଶୁଭ ନୁହେଁ ॥

Sakāḷu śejaru uṭhi je mukha nadhue | Tā mukha je jana dekhe tāra śubha nuhen ||

One who rises from bed in the morning but does not wash the face, | Anyone who sees that face will not experience auspiciousness.

ରାତ୍ରଶେଷେ ବାସିଶେଯେ ଯେ କରେ ଶୟନ । ତା ଗୃହକୁ ଲକ୍ଷ୍ମୀତ୍ୟାଗ କରନ୍ତି ବହନ ॥

Rātraśeṣe bāsiśeje je kare śayana | Tā gṛuhaku Lakṣmītyāga karanti bahana ||

One who sleeps on an unclean (used) bed at the end of night, | To that person's home, Lakshmi departs and does not reside.

ଆସନ ବିନା ଯେ ଭୂମିପରେ ବସି ଖାଏ । କିବା ଯେ କୁମାରୀ ସଙ୍ଗତରେ କାମମୋହେ ॥

Āsana binā je bhūmipare basi khāe | Kibā je kumārī saṅgatere kāmamohai ||

One who eats sitting directly on the ground without a seat, | Or who engages in lustful behaviour with an unmarried girl,

ଦକ୍ଷିଣ ପଶ୍ଚିମ ମୁଖେ ଯେ ଭୁଞ୍ଜି ବସଇ । ଏମାନଙ୍କ ପାଶୁ ଲକ୍ଷ୍ମୀ ଯାନ୍ତି ଦୂର ହୋଇ ॥

Dakṣiṇa paścima mukhe je bhuñji basai | Emānanka pāśu Lakṣmī jānti dūra hoi ||

One who eats facing the south or southwest direction, | From such people, Goddess Lakshmi departs and stays far away.

ସନ୍ଧ୍ୟାରେ କୁଣ୍ଢାଇ କେଶ ବାନ୍ଧେ ଯେଉନାରୀ । କେଭେ ନ ଦେଖନ୍ତି ଲକ୍ଷ ତାହାର ଯେ ଶିରୀ ॥

Sandhyāre kuṇḍhāi keśa bādhe jeu nārī | Kebhe na dekhanti lakṣa tāhāra je śirī ||

The woman who ties her hair into a knot during evening time, | Lakshmi never looks at her head (bestows no blessings).

ଭୋଜନକରି ଯେ ମୁଖ ଶୋଧନ ନ କରେ | ଭୋଜନ କରଇ ଯେହୁ ଅନ୍ଧକାର ଘରେ ॥

Bhojanakari je mukha śodhana na kare | Bhojana karai jehu andhakāra ghare ||

One who eats but does not clean their mouth afterward, | Or one who eats in a dark room without light,

ସ୍ନାନପରେ ହୁଅଇ ଯେ ତଇଲ ମରଦନ । କରେ ଯେହୁ ନଖମୁନେ ଭୂମି ବିଦାରଣ ॥

Snānapare huai je taila maradana | Kare jehu nakhamune bhūmi bidāraṇa ||

One who applies oil massage after bathing, | Or one who scratches and damages the ground with fingernails,

ପିନ୍ଧିଥିବ ଲୁଗା ଶେଷେ ଯେ ବିଞ୍ଚି ହୁଅଇ । ଏମାନଙ୍କ ବଦନକୁ ଲକ୍ଷ୍ମୀ ନ ଚାହାଁଇ ॥

Pindhithiba lugā śeṣe je biñci huai | Emānanka badanaku Lakṣmī na cānhai ||

One who fans herself using the end part of her worn clothes, | Goddess Lakshmi does not cast her glance on such a person.

ଯେଉଁ ନାରୀ ନିଜ ପତିଠାରେ ରୋଷବହେ । ସ୍ୱାମୀଯାହାବୋଲେ ତାହା ନକରେ କେବେହେଁ ॥

Jeun nārī nija patiṭhāre roṣabahe | Svāmījāhābole tāhā nakare kebehẽn ||

The woman who holds anger or resentment toward her own husband, | And never obeys what her husband says,

ପର ପୁରୁଷରେ ଯେହୁ ହୋଇଥାଏ ରତ । ପରିଷ୍ରୁତ ନୋହି ହୁଏ ଯେ ନାରୀ କୁତ୍ସିତ ॥

Para puruṣare jehu hoithāe rata | Pariṣṛuta nohi hue je nārī kutsita ||

A woman who is engaged in intimacy with another (non-husband) man, | Who is not pure (chaste), that woman is vile/disgraceful.

ଏମନ୍ତ ନାରୀଙ୍କ ମୁଖ ଲକ୍ଷ୍ମୀ ନ ଦେଖନ୍ତି । କାଙ୍ଗାଳିନୀ ପରି ବାରଦ୍ୱାରେ ସେ ବୁଲାନ୍ତି ॥

Emanta nārīṅka mukha Lakṣmī na dekhanti | Kāṅgāḷinī pari bāradvāre se bulānti ||

Goddess Lakshmi never sees the face of such a woman. | She roams from door to door like a beggar-woman.

କଳହୀ ଅଳସୀ ଅତି ଅପ୍ରିୟା ସାହସୀ । ଦେବ ବିପ୍ର ଅତିଥିରେ ନୁହଁଇ ବିଶ୍ୱାସୀ ॥

Kaḷahī alasī ati apriyā sāhasī | Deba vipra atithire nuhai viśvāsī ||

Quarrelsome, lazy, very unpleasant, and overly bold woman— | Who has no faith in gods, Brahmins, or guests,

ଏହିପରି ଯେଉଁନାରୀ ଥିଲେ ସେ ଗୃହଶ୍ମଶାନ । ଲକ୍ଷ୍ମୀ ସେ ସ୍ଥାନକୁ ସଦା କରନ୍ତି ବର୍ଜନ ॥

Ehipari jeun nārī thile se gṛuhaśmaśāna | Lakṣmī se sthānaku sadā karanti barjana ||

The house where such a woman lives becomes like a cremation ground. | Goddess Lakshmi always abandons such a place.

ଯେଉଁନାରୀ ଭକ୍ତିଚିତ୍ତେ ସ୍ୱାମୀକି ନ ସେବେ । ଜନ୍ମେଜନ୍ମେ ସ୍ୱାମୀଦୁଃଖେଦୁଃଖୀ ହୁଏ ଭବେ ॥

Jeun nārī bhakticitte svāmīki na sebe | Janmejanme svāmīduḥkhe duḥkhī hue bhabe ||

A woman who, even with devotion, does not serve her husband, | In every birth, she remains miserable due to suffering through her husband.

ଯେଉଁ ନାରୀ ସ୍ୱାମୀ କି ଦେବତା ସମମଣି | ସେବାକରି ତୋଷୁଥାଏ ତାର ମତି ଚିହ୍ନି ॥|

Jeun nārī svāmī ki devatā samamaṇi | Sebā kari toṣuthāe tāra mati cihni ||

The woman who considers her husband equal to a God, | Serves him and pleases him understanding his mindset (will),

ନିଜ ଅଙ୍ଗ ପରିଷ୍କାର କରି ଶୁଚି ହୁଏ । ସାନବଡ଼ ସମସ୍ତଙ୍କୁ ସମଭାବେ ଚାହେଁ ॥

Niḷa aṅga pariṣkāra kari śuci hue | Sānabaḍa samastaṅku samattābe cāhe ll

Bathing her body clean, she remains pure, | She respects both young and old equally with goodwill.

ପରଷିବା ବେଳେ ପକ୍ଷପାତ ଯେ ନକରେ । ସ୍ୱାମୀ ପୁତ୍ର ସମସ୍ତଙ୍କୁ ବାଣ୍ଟେ ସମାନରେ ॥

Paraṣibā beḷe pakṣapāta je nakare I Svāmī putra samastaṅku bāṇṭe samānare ll

While serving (food or duties), she never shows favouritism. | Distributes equally to husband, sons, and everyone.

ପତିର ଆଜ୍ଞାକୁ କେଭେ ନ ପକାଏ ତଳେ । ସ୍ୱାମୀଦୁଃଖେଦୁଃଖୀସୁଖେସୁଖୀହୋଇଚଳେ ॥

Patira ājñāku kebhe na pakāe taḷe I Svāmī-duḥkhe duḥkhī, sukhe sukhī hoi cale ll

Never disobeys or ignores her husband's command. | In her husband's sorrow, she is sorrowful; in his happiness, she rejoices.

ଏମନ୍ତ ନାରୀର ଗୃହ ଲକ୍ଷ୍ମୀ ନ ଛାଡ଼ନ୍ତି । ତାର ଦୁଃଖ ନୟନରେ କେବେ ନ ଦେଖନ୍ତି ॥

Emanta nārīra gṛuha Lakṣmī na chāḍanti I Tāra duḥkha nayanare kebe na dekhn̄ti II

Goddess Lakshmi never leaves the house of such a woman. | Her eyes never witness sorrow (she never suffers).

ଏ ମର୍ତ୍ତ୍ୟ ମଣ୍ଡଳେ ସେହି ନାରୀ ସୁଖପାଏ । ପତିପୁତ୍ରକନ୍ୟା ଅଇଶ୍ୱର୍ଯ୍ୟ ଯୁକ୍ତ ହୁଏ ॥

E martya maṇḍale sehi nārī sukhapāe I Pati-putra-kanyā aiśvarya yukta hue II

In this mortal world, such a woman attains happiness. | She is blessed with husband, sons, daughters, and prosperity.

ଅନ୍ତକାଳେ ବଇକୁଣ୍ଠେ ଲକ୍ଷ୍ମୀଙ୍କ ସଙ୍ଗରେ । ଅନୁକ୍ଷଣେ ମଜି ରହେ ପ୍ରମୋଦ ରଙ୍ଗରେ ॥

Antakāle Vaikuṇṭhe Lakṣmīṅka saṅgare I Anukṣaṇe maji rahe pramoda raṅgare II

At the end of life, she reaches Vaikuntha with Goddess Lakshmi. | Every moment, she remains immersed in joy and delight.

ସଧବା ନାରୀର ପତିବିନା ନାହିଁ ଗତି । ତପ ଜପ ଦେବ ପୂଜା ତାହାର ଅନୀତି ॥

Sadhabā nārīra patibinā nāhiṅ gati । Tapa japa deva pūjā tāhāra anīti ॥

For a married woman, without her husband, there is no (spiritual) progression. | All her penance, chants, and deity worship are considered improper (without husband's service).

ପତିସେବା ଛାଡ଼ି ବୃଥା ବ୍ରତ ଯେ କରଇ । ଜନ୍ମ ଜନ୍ମାନ୍ତରେ ବାଲ୍ୟ ବିଧବା ହୁଅଇ ॥

Pati-sevā chāḍi vṛuthā vrata je karai । Janma janmāntare bālya vidhavā huai ॥

The one who observes fasts and vows ignoring service to her husband, | She is born a widow in childhood across lifetimes.

ଯେଉଁ ନାରୀ ଆନନ୍ଦରେ ଅତିଥି ସେବଇ । ପୁଣ୍ୟବତୀ ବୋଲି ତାକୁ ପୁରାଣରେ କହି ॥

Jeuṅ nārī ānandare atithi sevai । Puṇyavatī boli tāku purāṇare kahi ॥

The woman who joyfully serves guests, | Is described as virtuous (punyavati) in the Puranas

ଏମନ୍ତ ପ୍ରକାରେ ଯେଉଁ ନାରୀ ବା ପୁରୁଷ । ଆପଣାର କୁଳଧର୍ମ ନ ଛାଡ଼ନ୍ତି ଲେଶ ॥

Emanta prakāre jeuṅ nārī bā puruṣa l Āpaṇāra kuladharma na chāḍanti leśa ll

Whoever, be it woman or man, | Never forsakes even a trace of their familial or traditional duty (kuladharma),

ସଦା ବେଳେ କରନ୍ତି ଉତ୍ତମ ଆଚରଣ । ଶ୍ରୀଲକ୍ଷ୍ମୀ ତାହାଙ୍କ ପାଦେ ମିଳନ୍ତି ତତ୍କ୍ଷଣ ॥

Sadā beḷe karanti uttama ācaraṇa l Śrī-Lakṣmī tāhāṅka pāde milaṅti tatkṣaṇa ll

Always follows noble conduct, | Goddess Lakshmi immediately resides at their feet (blesses them).

ପତିସେବା ବିନା ନାହିଁ ନାରୀଙ୍କର ଗତି । ପତିପ୍ରାଣା ନାରୀ କରେ ଦେବଲୋକ ଗତି ॥

Pati-sevā binā nāhiṅ nārīṅkara gati l Pati-prāṇā nārī kare devaloka gati ll

Without service to her husband, a woman has no path (salvation). | A woman who considers her husband as her life attains the realm of the Gods (heaven).

ନାରୀଙ୍କର ଲକ୍ଷ୍ମୀବ୍ରତ ପତିସେବା ବିନୀ । ଅନ୍ୟ ଦେବ ପୂଜ଼ାତୀର୍ଥ ଯାତ୍ରା ବିଡ଼ମ୍ବନା ॥

Nārīṅkara Lakṣmī-vrata pati-sevā binī I Anya deva pūjā tīrtha yātrā biḍambana II

A woman's Lakshmi Vrat (vow to Goddess Lakshmi) without serving her husband, | Worship of other deities or pilgrimage is just a mockery.

ପତିସେବା ବରଜି ଯେ ମାତି ଗରବରେ । ଗୁରୁବାରେ ଲକ୍ଷ୍ମୀବ୍ରତ ସେହୁ ଯଦି କରେ ॥

Pati-sevā baraji je māti garabare I Gurubāre Lakṣmī-vrata sehu jadi kare II

One who avoids serving her husband and is instead filled with pride, | Even if she performs Lakshmi Vrat on a Thursday,

ତାହାର ନୁହଇ ଭଲ ଜନମେ ଜନମେ | ଦୁଃଖ ଶୋକରୋଗଭୋଗସଂସାରେସେ ଭ୍ରମେ ॥

Tāhāra nuhai bhala janme janme I Duḥkha śoka roga bhoga sansāre se bhrame II

It is not good for her across births and lifetimes. | She wanders through worldly life suffering sorrow, disease, and hardship.

ଏମନ୍ତ ତିଆରି ସାଧବାଣୀକି କହିଲେ । ଆଜିଠାରୁ ଲକ୍ଷ୍ମୀବ୍ରତ କର ଯା ବୋଇଲେ ॥

Emanta tiāri sādhavāṇīki kahile । Ājiṭhāru Lakṣmī-vrata kara jā boile ॥

Thus, said to the housewife. | Begin observing Lakshmi Vrat from today onwards, she instructed.

ନ କଲେ ସର୍ବ ସମ୍ପଦ ତୋର କ୍ଷୟଯିବ । ଅନ୍ନ ବସ୍ତ୍ର ଅଭାବରେ ଦୁଃଖ ଭୋଗ ହେବ ॥

Na kale sarba sampada tora kṣaya jiba । Anna bastra abhābare duḥkha bhoga heba ॥

If you do not (follow), all your wealth will be destroyed. | You will suffer due to lack of food and clothing.

ଶୁଣ ହୋ ନାରଦ ଠାକୁରାଣୀ ଏହାକହି | ସେଠାବରୁ କେତେଦୂର ପଥ ଗଲେ ବାହି ॥

Śuṇa ho Nārada Ṭhākurāṇī ehā kahi । Sethābaru ketedūra patha gale bāhi ॥

Listen, O Narada, after saying this, the noble lady (Lakshmi) | Departed from there, going far along the road.

ଘରେ ଘରେ ପୁରେପୁରେ ଲକ୍ଷ୍ମୀ ବିଜେକଲେ । କାହାରି ଦୁଆରେ ସେହି ଶୁଚି ନ ଦେଖିଲେ ॥

Ghare ghare pure pure Lakṣmī bije kale I Kāhāra duāre sehi śuci na dekhile II

Lakshmi travelled through many houses and towns. | But at no one's door did she see that purity (cleanliness or righteousness).

କେବଣ ଯୁବତୀ ନିଦେ ହୋଇ ଅଚେତନ | କାହାର ଫିଟିଯାଇଛି ପିନ୍ଧିଲା ବସନ ॥

Kebaṇa juvatī nide hoi acetana I Kāhāra phiṭi jāichi pindhilā vasana II

Some young women were seen lying unconscious in sleep, | Some had worn untied or dishevelled clothes.

କାହାର ଶରରେ କେଶ ମୁକୁଳିତ ହୋଇ | ଭୂମିପରେ ପଡ଼ିଅଛି କେରି କେରି ହୋଇ ॥

Kāhāra śarare keśa mukulita hoi I Bhūmi-pare paḍi achi keri keri hoi II

On someone's body, the hair was dishevelled (unkempt and loose), | Lying on the ground in a scattered and messy state.

ଏହିରୂପେ ମହାଲକ୍ଷ୍ମୀ ଦେଖିକରି ଗଲେ । ଚଣ୍ଡାଳ ସାହିରେ ଯାଇଁ ପ୍ରବେଶ ହୋଇଲେ ॥

Eharūpe Mahālakṣmī dekhi kari gale I Caṇḍāla sāhire jāin prabeśa hoile II

Seeing this condition, Mahalakshmi left that place. | She went and entered into the neighbourhood of the outcastes (Chandala community).

ଶ୍ରୀୟା ଚଣ୍ଡାଲୁଣୀ ନଗ୍ର ବାହାରେ ତା ଘର | ତାହାର ମହିମା ଯେ ଦେବଙ୍କୁ ଅଗୋଚର ॥

Śrīyā Caṇḍāluṇī nagra bāhāre tā ghara I Tāhāra mahimā je debāṅku agochara II

Shriya the Chandaluni (female outcaste) lived in a house outside the city. | Her glory was such that even the Gods were unaware (hidden from divine knowledge).

ପ୍ରତିଦିନ ଖରକଇ ଗୁଣ୍ଡିଚା ନଗର । ବିଷ୍ଣୁ ଭକତିରେ ସେ ଯେ ଅତି ତତପର ॥

Pratidina kharakai Guṇḍicā nagara I Vishnu bhaktire se je ati tatpara II

Every day, she swept (cleaned) the Gundicha city. | She was extremely devoted to Vishnu (deeply engaged in Vishnu's devotion).

ରାତ୍ର ବେନି ଘଡ଼ି ଥାଇ ଚଣ୍ଡାଲୁଣୀ ଗଲା । ଏକ ବର୍ଣ୍ଣ ଗାଈର ଯେ ଗୋବର ଆଣିଲା ॥

Rātra beni ghaḍi thāi Caṇḍāluṇī galā । Eka varṇa gāīra je gobara ānilā ॥

At night, as the braiding hour (around late night) arrived, the Chandali woman went (out). | She brought cow dung from one coloured (sacred) cow.

ଉତ୍ତମ କରିଣ ଘରଦ୍ୱାରକୁ ଲିପିଲା । ଛଡ଼ାପାଣି ମୁନ୍ଦାଏ ଦୁଆରେ ପକାଇଲା ॥

Uttama kariṇa gharadvāraku lipilā । Chaḍāpāṇi mundāe duāre pakāilā ॥

She excellently smeared (purified) the house and doorway. | She sprinkled (holy) water at the doorway (i.e., as a traditional ritual).

ଅରୁଆ ଚାଉଳ ବାଟି ଘରେ ଝୋଟି ଦେଲା ।ଷୋଳକୋଠି କରି ଦିବ୍ୟ ପଦ୍ମେକ କାଟିଲା ॥

Aruā cāuḷa bāṭi ghare jhoṭi delā । Ṣoḷa-koṭhi kari dibya padmeka kāṭilā ॥

She ground raw rice and decorated the house (made alpana/mandala). | She formed a sixteen-petalled divine lotus design (in the decoration).

ଦଶମୁଖୀ ଦୀପାବଳୀ ମଣ୍ଡଳେ ଥୋଇଲା । ଦଶବର୍ଣ୍ଣ ଫଳମୂଳ ମଣ୍ଡଳେ ବାଢ଼ିଲା ॥

Daśamukhī Dīpābalī maṇḍale thoilā । Daśabarṇa phala-mūla maṇḍale bāḍhilā ॥

She placed a ten-faced row of lamps within the mandala (decorative circle). | She arranged ten types of fruits and roots within the mandala.

ସୁତା ଦଶଖିଅ ନେଇ ମଣ୍ଡଳେ ଥୋଇଲା । ମନର ଚଞ୍ଚଳେ ପୁଣି ବେଗେ ଚଳିଗଲା ॥

Sutā daśakhia nei maṇḍale thoilā । Manara cañcale puṇi bege caligalā ॥

She placed ten cotton threads within the mandala. | With a restless mind (or with a devotional urge), she quickly went away again.

ଅରୁଆ ଚାଉଳ ଆଉ ଦୁବ ଦଶକେରା । ତାହା ନେଇ ଚଣ୍ଡାଳୁଣୀ ମଣ୍ଡଳେ ଥୋଇଲା ॥

Aruā cāuḷa āu duba daśakerā । Tāhā nei Caṇḍāḷuṇī maṇḍale thoilā ॥

Raw rice and ten blades of sacred grass (dubo grass). | Taking those, the Chandali woman placed them in the mandala.

ଧୂପଦୀପ ନଇବେଦ୍ୟ ଗନ୍ଧପୁଷ୍ପ ଦେଲା । ଲକ୍ଷ୍ମୀନାରାୟଣ ବୋଲି ସୁମରଣା କଲା ॥

Dhūpadīpa naibedya gandhapuṣpa delā I Lakṣmīnārāyaṇa boli sumaraṇā kalā II

She offered incense, lamp, food offerings, and fragrant flowers. | Chanting "Lakshmi-Narayana," she began to remember (invoke) them.

ନମସ୍ତେ ନମସ୍ତେ ମାଗୋ ହରିଙ୍କ ଘରଣୀ । ମୁହିଁଛାର ହୀନଜାତି ନ ଜାଣଇ ପୁଣି ॥

Namaste namaste māgo Hariṅka gharaṇī I Muhiñchhāra hīnajāti na jāṇai puṇI II

Salutations, salutations, O Mother, consort of Lord Hari. | I am of low birth, ignorant and untaught in proper rituals.

ଚଣ୍ଡାଳ ସାହିରେ ଘର ପୂଣି ଚଣ୍ଡାଳୁଣୀ | କିଞ୍ଚିତେ ଭକତି ମୋର ଘେନ କମଳିନୀ ॥

Caṇḍāḷa sāhire ghara pūṇi Caṇḍāḷuṇī I Kiñcite bhakati mora ghena Kamaḷinī II

A Chandali woman with a house in the untouchable colony. | Yet I have a little devotion in my heart, O lotus-dweller (Lakshmi).

ଦାଣ୍ଡେ ଦାଣ୍ଡେ ଯାଉଥିଲେ ବିଷ୍ଣୁ ପାଟରାଣୀ । ସହି ନ ପାରିଲେ ଚଣ୍ଡାଲୁଣୀର ଦୟିନୀ ॥

Dāṇḍe dāṇḍe jāuthile Vishnu pāṭarāṇī I Sahi na pārile Caṇḍāḷuṇīra dayinī II

As Queen Lakshmi of Vishnu was walking from house to house... | ...she could not bear the compassion (devotion) of the Chandali woman.

ପଦ୍ମଫୁଲ ଦେଖି ତାଙ୍କ ଚଳିଲା ଶରଧା । ଦୁଇପାଦ ଦେଇ ମାତା ପଦ୍ମେ ହେଲେ ଉଭା ॥

Padmaphula dekhi tāṅka calilā śaradhā I Duipāda dei mātā padme hele ubhā II

Seeing the lotus flower, her faith was stirred. | The Mother (Lakshmi) stood with both feet on the lotus.

ଚଣ୍ଡାଲୁଣୀ ଘରଗୋଟି ପାଇଲାକ ଶୋଭା । ଲକ୍ଷ୍ମୀ ବିଜେ କରିଛନ୍ତି କି ଉପମା ଦେବା ॥

Caṇḍāḷuṇī gharagoṭi pāilāka śobhā I Lakṣmī bije karichanti ki upamā debā II

The Chandali woman's single house received divine beauty. | Lakshmi has graced it—what comparison can be given?

ବୋଇଲେ ଲୋ ଚଣ୍ଡାଲୁଣୀମାଗି ଘେନବର। ପ୍ରସନ୍ନ ହୋଇଲି ଦୁଃଖ ନାଶିବ ତୋହର ॥

Boile lo Caṇḍāḷuṇīmāgi ghena bara I Prasanna hoili duḥkha nāśiba tohara II

Lakshmi said, "Listen, O Chandāli, ask and receive a boon!" | "I am pleased; your sorrows shall be destroyed."

ଚଣାଲୁଣୀ କହୁଅଛି ଶିରେ କର ଦେଇ | କି ବର ମାଗିବି ମାଗୋ ମାଗି ନ ଜାଣଇ ॥

Caṇḍāḷuṇī kahuachhi śire kara dei I Ki vara māgibi māgo māgi na jāṇai II

The Chandali said, placing her hand on her head: | "What boon should I ask, O Mother? I do not know what to ask."

ଗୋ-ଗୋଷ୍ଠକୁ ଦେବ ମୋର ଲକ୍ଷ୍ମେପଦ୍ମ ଗାଈ । କୁବେର ସମାନ ଧନ ଦେବୁ ମାତ ତୁହି ॥

Go-goṣṭhaku deba mora Lakṣmepadma gāī I Kubera samāna dhana debu māta tuhi II

"Please give a cow for my cowshed, O Lakshmi-lotus!" | "O Mother, may you give me wealth like Kubera's!"

କୋଳକୁ ନନ୍ଦନ ଯେ ହସ୍ତକୁ ସୁନାବାହି । ଚାରିଯୁଗେ ବସିବି ଅମର ବର ପାଇ ॥

Koḷaku nandana je hastaku sunābāhī I Cārijuge basibi amara vara pāi II

"A child in my lap, and golden bangles on my hand (wrist). | I should live through the four ages, having received the boon of immortality."

ଲକ୍ଷ୍ମୀ ଶୁଣି ବୋଇଲେ ତୁ ହୋଇଛୁ କି ବାଇ । ଏ ସମସ୍ତ ବର ତୋତେ ଦେଇତ ପାରଇ ॥

Lakṣmī śuṇi boile tu hoichhu ki bāi I E samasta vara toṭe deita pārai II

Hearing this, Lakshmi said, "Are you out of your mind!" | "I am able to give you all these boons."

ଅମର ବର ଦେବାକୁ ଶକ୍ତି ମୋର ନାହିଁ । ଏହି ବର ମାଗିଲୁ ତୁ କେମନ୍ତ ପ୍ରକାର ॥

Amara vara debāku śakti mora nāhiṅ I Ehi vara māgilū tu kemanta prakāra II

"But I do not have the power to grant the boon of immortality." | "Why and how did you ask for such a boon?"

ଯେତେ ଦିନ ଜୀଇଥିବୁ ଐଶ୍ୱର୍ଯ୍ୟ ଭୁଞ୍ଜିବୁ । ଅନ୍ତକାଳେ ଯାଇ ବିଷ୍ଣୁ ପଞ୍ଜରେ ପଶିବୁ ॥

Jete dina jīithibu aiśvarya bhuñjibu I Antakāle jāi Vishnu pañjare paśibu II

As long as you live, you will enjoy prosperity. | At the end of life, you will enter into the abode of Lord Vishnu.

ମୋହର ଏ ବ୍ରତ କରିଥିବୁ ସବୁଦିନ । ଲକ୍ଷ୍ମୀନାରାୟଣ ପାଦେ ଥିବ ତୋର ମନ ॥

Mohara e vrata karithibu sabudina I Lakṣmīnārāyaṇa pāde thiba tora mana II

If you observe this vow of mine all your life... | ...then may your heart remain at the feet of Lakshmi-Narayana.

ଶୁଣ ହେ ନାରଦ ଏଣେ ହରି ବଳରାମ । ମୃଗୟା ବିନୋଦେ ଯାଇଥିଲେ ଘୋରବନ ॥

Śuṇa he Nārada eṇe Hari Balarāma I Mṛugaya binode jāithile ghorabana II

Listen, O Narada, Hari and Balaram... | ...went for hunting amusement in a deep forest.

ଯୋଗବଳେ ବଳରାମ ଏ କଥା ଜାଣିଲେ । ଡାକି ହରି ଶ୍ରୀହରିଙ୍କୁ ଏମନ୍ତ କହିଲେ ॥

Jogabaḷe Balarāma e kathā jāṇile I Ḍāki Hari Srihariṅku emanta kahile II

Through yogic power, Balaram came to know this matter. | Calling Hari (Krishna), he spoke thus to Narayan-Hari.

ଦେଖ ଦେଖ କହ୍ନାଇ ତୋ ଭାରିଯା ଆଚାର । ଉଭା ହୋଇ ଅଛଇ ଯେ ଚଣ୍ଡାଳୁଣୀ ଘର ॥

Dekha dekha Kahnāi to bhārijā ācāra I Ubha hoi achhai je Caṇḍāḷuṇī ghara II

"Look, look Kanhaiya! What improper behaviour your wife has!" | The house of a Chandali (low-caste woman) is where Lakshmi is standing.

ହାଡ଼ି ଘରେ ଥିବ ଲକ୍ଷ୍ମୀ ପାଣ ଘରେ ଥିବ । ସ୍ନାନ ନ କରିଣ ବଡ଼ଦେଉଳେ ପଶିବ ॥

Hāḍi ghare thiba Lakṣmī pāṇa ghare thiba I Snāna na kariṇa baḍadeuḷe paśiba II

Lakshmi is visiting Hadi and Pana (low-caste) houses (termed Impure). | Without bathing, she enters the grand temple.

ଏହି ରୂପେ ସବୁଦିନେ ଦେଉଳେ ପଶୁଛି । ଦୁଇଗୋଟି ଭାଇଙ୍କୁ ବିଟାଳ କରାଉଛି ॥

Ehi rūpe sabudine deuḷe paśuchhi । Duigoṭi bhāiṅku biṭāḷa karāuchhi ॥

In this way, every day she enters the temple. | And She is creating disturbance for the two brothers.

ଦରିଦ୍ର ଭଞ୍ଜନୀ ନାମ ଯେଣୁ ଅଛି ବହି । ଦରିଦ୍ରମାନଙ୍କ କଷ୍ଟ ନ ପାରଇ ସହି ॥

Daridra bhañjanī nāma jeṇu achhi bahi । Daridramānaṅka kaṣṭa na pārai sahī ॥

"Daridra Bhanjani" (Destroyer of Poverty) is the name found in the scriptures. | She cannot bear the suffering of the poor.

ସୂଦଶା ନାମରେ ଏକ ବ୍ରତ ଯେ ତାହାର | ଏହି ବ୍ରତେ ଚଣ୍ଡାଲୁଣୀ ପୂଜଇ ପୟର ॥

Sūdaśā nāmare eka vrata je tāhāra । Ehi brate Caṇḍāḷuṇī pūjai payara ॥

There is a vrata (vow/ritual) of Hers called "Sudasha." | In this vow, even a Chandali woman worships with devotion.

ଭାରିଯାରେ କାର୍ଯ୍ୟଯେବେ ଅଛିରେ କହ୍ନାଇ ।ଚଣ୍ଡାଳ ସାହିରେ ନଗ୍ର ତୋଳ ବେଗେ ଯାଇ॥

Bhārijāre kāryajebe achhire Kahnāi । Caṇḍāḷa sāhire nagra toḷa bege jāi ॥

"If you are supporting your wife, Kanhaiya (Krishna)..." | "Go quickly and build a house in the Chandala neighbourhood."

ଆମ୍ଭ ବାକ୍ୟ ମାନି ତାକୁ ଦିଅ ଘଉଡ଼ାଇ । ଏପରି ଘରଣୀ ଥିଲେ ଭଲ ଗତି ନାହିଁ ॥

Āmbha bākya māni tāku dia ghaudāi । Epari gharaṇī thile bhaḷa gati nāhiṅ ॥

Follow my command and drive Her out of the temple. | If such a housewife exists, it is inevitable to have ill fate.

ଗୋବିନ୍ଦ ବୋଇଲେ ଭାଇ ଘଉଡ଼ାଇ ଦେବା । ଲକ୍ଷ୍ମୀପରା ଭାରିଯାକୁ ଆଉ ନ ପାଇବା ॥

Govinda boile bhāi ghaurdāi debā । Lakṣmīparā bhārijāku āu na pāibā ॥

Govinda said, "Brother, we must drive Her out of the temple | But a wife like Lakshmi — we will not find another."

ସେ ଯେବେ ଦୋଷ କରିଛି ଏମନ୍ତ କରିବା । ସ୍ୱର୍ଗ ପୁର ଲୋକଙ୍କୁ ଡକାଇ ଅଣାଇବା ॥

Se jebe doṣa karichhi emanta karibā I Svarga pura lokaṅku ḍakāi aṇāibā II

"When She has committed a fault, we will take such an action." | "We will summon the people of heaven and bring them."

ପାଞ୍ଚଲକ୍ଷ ଟଙ୍କାଦେଇ ଜାତି କରାଇବା । ଆଉ ବେଳେ ତାର ଯଦି ଅନୀତି ଦେଖିବା ॥

Pāñcalakṣa ṭaṅkādei jāti karāibā I Āu beḷe tāra jadi anīti dekhībā II

"We will pay five lakh coins and purify her caste (restore honour)." | "But if ever we see any wrongdoings from Her again..."

ଦେଉଳ ଭିତରୁ ତାକୁ ଦେବା ଘଉଡ଼ାଇ । ଏକଥା ପ୍ରମାଣ ତୁମ୍ଭେ ଶୁଣ ଜ୍ୟେଷ୍ଠଭାଇ ॥

Deuḷa bhitaru tāku debā ghaurdāi I Ekathā pramāṇa tumbhe śuṇa jyeṣṭhabhāi II

"We will drive Her out of the temple with turmeric (symbolically cast her out)." | "Let this be the proof—listen, elder brother!"

ନ ଜାଣି ଯେ ଦୋଷକଲେ ସିନ୍ଧୁ ରାଜଜେମା | ବାରେ ମାତ୍ର ଭାଇ ତାଙ୍କ ଦୋଷକର କ୍ଷମା ॥

Na jāṇi je doṣakale sindhu rājajemā | Bāre mātra bhāi tāṅka doṣakara kṣamā ll

Not knowing, Sindhu Rājajemā (Queen of Sindhu) committed a mistake. | At least this time, Brother, forgive Her fault.

ବଳରାମ ବୋଲୁଛନ୍ତି ଶୁଣ ଭାବଗ୍ରାହୀ । ତୋର ଲକ୍ଷ୍ମୀଥିଲେ ମୁହିଁ ରହିବଇଁ ନାହିଁ ॥

Baḷarāma boluchanti śuṇa bhābagrāhī | Tora lakṣmīthile muhin rahibain nāhin ll

Balaram says, "Listen, you who understand emotions." | "If your Lakshmi stays here, then I will no longer stay."

ଭାରିଯା ଅଟଇ ସିନା ପାଦର ପାଣ୍ଡୋଇ | ଭାଇଥିଲେ କୋଟିଭାର୍ଯ୍ୟା ମିଳି ଯେ ପାରଇ ॥

Bhārijā aṭai sinā pādara pāṇḍoī | Bhāithile koṭibhārjyā miḷi je pārai ll

The wife is just like the sacred white sandal paste at the feet. | If you have a brother, you can get a crore wives.

ଭାର୍ଯ୍ୟାଠାରେ ଲୋଭ ଯେବେ ଅଛିରେ କହ୍ନାଇ | ଚଣ୍ଡାଳ ସାହିରେ ତୁ ନଅର ତୋଳ ଯାଇ ॥

Bhārjyāṭhāre lobha jebe achire kahnāi | Caṇḍāḷa sāhire tu na'ara toḷa jāi ll

"O Krishna, when there is desire (greed) for a wife..." | "...you go and build a house in a Chandala's lane!"

ମୋର ବଡ଼ ଦେଉଳକୁ ଆଉ ନ ଆସିବୁ | ମାଇପକୁ ଘେନି ଦାଣ୍ଡ ବାହାରେ ରହିବୁ ॥

Mora baḍa deūḷaku ā'u na āsibu | Māipaku ghēni dāṇda bāhāre rahibu ll

"Do not come to my main temple again." | "Stay outside the door, with your wife (Lakshmi)."

ଧିକ୍କାର ବଚନ ପ୍ରଭୁ ସହି ନ ପାରିଲେ । ଛାଡ଼ିଲି ବୋଲିଣ ରଙ୍ଗ ଅଧର କହିଲେ ॥

Dhikkāra bacana prabhu sahi na pārile | Chāḍili boḷiṇa raṅga adhara kahile ll

The Lord could not bear the words of reproach. | He stopped speaking, and the colour of His lips faded.

ଦେଉଳର ସିଂହଦ୍ୱାରେ ପ୍ରବେଶ ହୋଇଲେ । ଊର୍ଦ୍ଧ୍ୱମୁଖ ହୋଇ ପ୍ରଭୁ ନିଶ୍ୱାସ ଛାଡ଼ିଲେ ॥

Deūḷara sinhadvāre prabeśa hoile | Ūrdhvamukha hoi prabhu niśvāsa chāḍile ||

He entered through the lion-gate of the temple. | With face turned upward, the Lord sighed deeply.

ଶୁଣ ହେ ନାରଦ ତେଣେ ଶ୍ରୀୟା ଚଣ୍ଡାଳୁଣୀ । ପୂଜା କରୁଥଲା ଲକ୍ଷ୍ମୀଙ୍କର ପାଦବେନି ॥

Śuṇa he nārada teṇe śrīyā caṇḍāluṇī | Pūjā karuthalā Lakṣmīṅkara pādabeni ||

Listen, O Narada! That Chandala woman named Shriya... | ...was worshipping the feet of Goddess Lakshmi.

ତାହାର ପୂଜାରେ ଦେବୀ ସନ୍ତୁଷ୍ଟ ହୋଇଲେ । ଯାଚିଣ ଅନେକ ବର ପ୍ରଦାନ ଯେ କଲେ ॥

Tāhāra pūjāre Devī santuṣṭa hoile | Jāciṇa aneka bara pradāna je kale ||

The Goddess became pleased with her worship. | Upon request, the Goddess granted her many boons.

କୁଟୀର ଖଣ୍ଡିକ ଥିଲା ବଲୁରିର ବାସ । ଲକ୍ଷ୍ମୀ ଦୟାକଲେ ତାକୁ ଚନ୍ଦନ ଉଆସ ॥

Kuṭīra khaṇḍika thulā balurira bāsa | Lakṣmī dayākale tāku candana uāsa ll

The broken hut of sand where she lived... | ...was turned into a palace of sandalwood by Lakshmi's grace.

ଯେଉଁ ଚଣ୍ଡାଲୁଣୀ ଘରେ ନ ଥିଲାକ ଅନ୍ନ | ଚାରିକୋଣେ ଦେଲେ ତାକୁ ଶୁଦ୍ଧ ଯେ ସୁବର୍ଣ୍ଣ ॥

Jeun caṇḍāluṇī ghare na thilāka anna | Cārikōṇe dele tāku śuddha je subarṇa ll

In the house of that Chandala woman where there was no food, | In all four corners (of the house), pure gold was bestowed upon her.

ଯେଉଁ ଚଣ୍ଡାଲୁଣୀ ଘରେ ନ ଥିଲାକ ପୁତ୍ର | ଲକ୍ଷ୍ମୀଦୟା କଲେ ତାର ହେଲା ପାଞ୍ଚସୁତ ॥

Jeun caṇḍāluṇī ghare na thilāka putra | Lakṣmīdayā kale tāra helā pāñcasuta ll

In the house of that Chandala woman where there was no son, | By Lakshmi's grace, she was blessed with five sons.

ଧନ ପୁତ୍ରବତୀ ହୁଅ ବୋଲିଣ ବୋଇଲେ । ବରଦେଇ ସେଠାବରୁ ବିଜେ କରିଗଲେ ॥

Dhana putravatī hua boḷiṇa boile | Baradei seṭhābaru bije karigale ll

Lakshmi said, "May you be blessed with wealth and sons." | Giving boons, she then departed in victory from that place.

ଲକ୍ଷ୍ମୀହେତୁ ଚଣ୍ଡାଲୁଣୀ ହେଲା ଭାଗ୍ୟବତୀ । ଏବେ ଶୁଣ ହେ ନାରଦ ଅପୂର୍ବ ଭାରତୀ ॥

Lakṣmīhetu caṇḍāluṇī helā bhāgyavatī | Ebe śūṇa he nārada apūrva bhāratī ll

Because of Lakshmi, the Chandala woman became fortunate. | Now listen, O Narada, to this extraordinary narrative.

ସିଂହଦ୍ୱାରେ ବିଜୟ ଲକ୍ଷ୍ମୀ ଯେ ମହାମାୟୀ । ଦେଖିଲେ ଦୁଆରେ ବସିଛନ୍ତି ବେନିଭାଇ ॥

Sinhadvāre vijaya lakṣmī je mahāmāyī | Dekhile duāre basichanti benibhāi ll

At the lion-gate stands the victorious Lakshmi, the great enchantress. | And she saw both the brothers sitting at the door.

ବୋଇଲେ ଯେ ବାଟ ଛାଡ଼ ଭିତରକୁ ଯିବି । ଦଶମୀ ଯୋଗାଡ଼ ମୁହିଁ ମଣୋହୀ ରାନ୍ଧିବି ॥

Boile je bāṭa chāḍa bhitaraku jibi | Daśamī jogāḍa muhin maṇohī rāndhibi ll

She (Lakshmi) said, "I shall leave the road and go inside (the house)." | "I will cook delicious food for the Dashami (the sacred tenth day)."

ଗୋବିନ୍ଦ ବୋଇଲେ ଲକ୍ଷ୍ମୀ ହୋଇଲ କି ବାଇ । ଚଣ୍ଡାଳ ସାହିକି ଯାଇଥିଲ କାହିଁ ପାଇଁ ॥

Gobinda boile lakṣmī hoila ki bāi | Caṇḍāḷa sāhiki jāithila kāhin pāin ll

Govinda (Krishna) said, "Lakshmi, what has happened to you, woman?" | "Why did you go to the Chandala's (untouchable's) settlement?"

ଆମ୍ଭେ ନ ଦେଖୁଣୁ ଯେ ଦେଖିଲେ ବଡ଼ ଭାଇ । ଆମ୍ଭେ ଦେଖିଥିଲେ ସିନା ଦିଅନ୍ତୁ ଘୋଡ଼ାଇ ॥

Āmbhe na dekhunu je dekhile baḍa bhāi | Āmbhe dekithile sinā diantu ghodāi ll

"Though I did not see it, the elder brother saw it." | "Had I seen it, I would have hidden your action."

ଯାଅ ଲକ୍ଷ୍ମୀ ତୁମ୍ଭଠାରେ ଆଉ କାର୍ଯ୍ୟ ନାହିଁ । ଧିକ୍କାର ବହୁତ ମୋତେ କଲେ ବଡ଼ଭାଇ ॥

Jā'a Lakṣmī tumbhathāre ā'u kārya nāhin | Dhikkāra bahuta mote kale baḍabhāi ll

"Go, Lakshmi — there is no more use for you here!" | "Elder brother has greatly insulted me!"

ହାଡ଼ିଘରେ ଥିବ ଲକ୍ଷ୍ମୀ ଥିବ ପାଣଘରେ | ସ୍ନାନ ନ କରି ପଶୁଛି ଦେଉଳ ଭିତରେ ॥

Hāḍighare thiba Lakṣmī thiba pāṇaghara | Snāna na kari paśuchi deūḷa bhitare ll

"Lakshmi is visiting Hadi and Pana houses (low-caste settlement)," | "Yet (She) enters the temple without even taking a bath!"

ତା'ଠାରୁ ପାପିନୀ ଆଉ ସଂସାରରେ ନାହିଁ | ମୋହର ବଚନ ଏବେ ଶୁଣ ପ୍ରାଣସହୀ ॥

Tā'ṭhāru pāpinī ā'u sansārare nāhin | Mohara bacana ebe śuṇa prāṇasahī ll

There is no greater sinner than You in this world. | Now listen to my words, O beloved companion of my life.

ଜଗତେ ବୋଲନ୍ତି ତୋତେ ବାଇ ଠାକୁରାଣୀ | ବାଇପ୍ରାୟ ବୁଲୁଥାଉ ହୋଇ ମୋ ଘରଣୀ ॥

Jagate bolanti tote bāi ṭhākurāṇī | Bāiprāya buluthāu hoi mo gharaṇī ll

People in the world call you a mistress, a queen. | But you roam around like a courtesan, even though you are my wife.

ଏକ ଘର କରାଉ ସହସ୍ର ଘରଭାଙ୍ଗି । ସହସ୍ର ଘର କରାଉ ଏକଘର ଭାଙ୍ଗି ॥

Eka ghara karā'u sahasra gharabhāṅgi | Sahasra ghara karā'u ekaghara bhāṅgi ll

You make one house by breaking a thousand others. | And you make a thousand homes by destroying just one.

ଏମନ୍ତ ପ୍ରକାର ଲକ୍ଷ୍ମୀ ମହିମା ତୋହର | ଯାଅ ଲକ୍ଷ୍ମୀ ବାହାରି ଗୋ ନ ରହ ମୋ ପୁର ॥

Emanta prakāra Lakṣmī mahimā tohara | Jā'a Lakṣmī bāhāri go na raha mo pura ll

Such is your glory, O Lakshmi! | Go, Lakshmi — leave now, do not stay in my city any longer.

ତୋହଠାରେ କୋପ କରିଛନ୍ତି ଜ୍ୟେଷ୍ଠଭାଇ । ଲକ୍ଷ୍ମୀଦେବୀ କହୁଛନ୍ତି ଠାକୁରଙ୍କୁ ଚାହିଁ ॥

Tohaṭhāre kōpa karichanti jyēṣṭhabhāi | Lakṣmīdevī kahuchanti ṭhākuraṅku cāhin ll

Your elder brother is angry with you. | Goddess Lakshmi says this, looking at the Lord.

ଛାଡ଼ପତ୍ର ଦେଇ ମୋତେ ଦିଅ ଘଉଡ଼ାଇ । ଜଗନ୍ନାଥ କହୁଛନ୍ତି ଲକ୍ଷ୍ମୀମୁଖ ଚାହିଁ ॥

Chāḍapatra dei mote di'a gha'uḍāi | Jagannātha kahuchanti lakṣmīmukha cāhin ll

"Give me a formal separation (divorce) letter and banish me." | Lord Jagannath speaks while looking at Lakshmi's face.

ଆମ୍ଭ ଜାତିରେ ତ ଛାଡ଼ପତ୍ର ଚଳେ ନାହିଁ । ଛାଡ଼ିବା ଭାରିଜା ମୁଖ ଚାହିଁ ନ ଯୋଗାଇ ॥

Āmbha jātire ta chāḍapatra cale nāhin | Chāḍibā bhārijā mukha cāhin na jogā'i ll

In our tradition, formal separation letters are not practiced. | I cannot bear to see my wife's face to say goodbye and leave.

ଲକ୍ଷ୍ମୀଦେବୀ କହୁଛନ୍ତି ଠାକୁରଙ୍କୁ ଚାହିଁ । ଯେତେବେଳେ ସାଗର ମନ୍ଥିଲେ ଦେବଯାଇ ॥

Lakṣmīdevī kahuchanti ṭhākuraṅku cāhin | Jetebeḷe sāgara manthile debajā'i ॥

Goddess Lakshmi says to the Lord, looking directly at Him: | When the ocean was churned, all the Gods had gone there...

ବେଦମନ୍ତ୍ରାଦି ସହିତେ ମୋତେ ପାଇଥିଲ | ସେତେବେଳ କଥାତୁମ୍ଭେ ପାଶୋରି ଯେ ଦେଲ ॥

Bedamantādi sahite mote pāithila | Setebeḷa kathātumbhe pāśori je dela ॥

You received me (married me) amidst Vedic chants and mantras. | At that time, you gave your promises (vows) in front of witnesses.

ମୋର ପିତା ବରୁଣ ଯେ ତୁମ୍ଭଙ୍କୁ ବରିଲେ | କନକବେଦୀରେ ନେଇ ବିଭା କରାଇଲେ ॥

Mora pitā varuṇa je tumbhaṅku barile | Kanakabedīre nei bibhā karāile ॥

My father Varuna chose you (as my husband). | On a golden altar, he arranged our wedding ceremony.

ଝିଅ ଦେଇ ଶରଣ ପଶିଲେ ତୁମ୍ଭଠାଇଁ । ଦଶଦୋଷ ମୋର କ୍ଷମା କରିବାର ପାଇଁ ॥

Jhiā dei śaraṇa paśile tumbhaṭhāin | Daśadoṣa mora kṣamā karibāra pāin ||

He gave his daughter (me) and surrendered to you. | (He did so) asking you to forgive any ten faults of mine.

ଦଶଗୋଟି ଦୋଷରୁ ଗୋଟିଏ ନ ସହିଲ | ପ୍ରଥମରେ ଚଣ୍ଡାଲୁଣି ବୋଲି ଗାଳିଦେଲ ॥

Daśagoṭi doṣaru goṭie na sahila | Prathamare caṇḍāluṇi boli gālidela ||

Out of ten faults, you couldn't tolerate even one. | For my first fault, you abused me, calling me "chandaluṇi" (outcaste woman).

ବିଭା ବାସୀଦିନ ଜୁଆ ଖେଳିବାର ବେଳେ | ସାତକଡ଼ା କଉଡ଼ି ଯେ ପାତିଲଇଁ ତଳେ ॥

Bibhā bāsīdina juā kheḷibāra beḷe | Sātakaḍā ka'uḍi je pātilain taḷe ||

On the very next day after the wedding, during the gambling session, | You scattered a hundred cowries upon the ground.

ତୁମ୍ଭେ ଢାଳିଦିଅ ନାଥ ମୋହର ହସ୍ତରେ । ସୁବର୍ଣ୍ଣ କଉଡ଼ି ମୁହିଁ ଜାକିଲଇଁ କରେ ॥

Tumbhe dhāḷidi'a nātha mohar hastare | Subarṇa ka'uḍi muhin jākilain kare ||

You, O Lord, had poured (cast) into my hands — | The golden cowries (coins) which I then held and jingled (as a sign of wealth).

ଛଡ଼ାଇ ନ ପାରି ତୁମେ ବ୍ରହ୍ମାଣ୍ଡ ଠାକୁର | ମୋତେ ବୋଇଲ ଯା'ଇଛା ମାଗିଘେନ ବର ॥

Chadā'i na pāri tume brahmāṇḍa ṭhākura | Mote boila jā'ichā māgighena bara ||

I am unable to forsake you, O Lord of the universe. | You told me to go and ask for a boon.

ଯାହା ମନ ବାଞ୍ଛା ଗୋ କରିବୁ ବଇଦେହୀ | ତାହା ମୁଁ ଅବଶ୍ୟ ଦେବି ଶୁଣ ପ୍ରାଣସହୀ ॥

JĀHĀ mana bāñcā go karibu baidehī | Tāhā muṁ avaśya debi śuṇa prāṇasahī ||

Whatever desire you have in your mind, O Vaidehi (a term addressing the Goddess), | I will surely give it to you — listen, O soul-companion (dear one).

କରପତ୍ର ଯୋଡ଼ିଣ ମୁଁ ବୋଇଲି ଉତ୍ତର । ସାବଧାନ ହୋଇ ଶୁଣ ବ୍ରହ୍ମାଣ୍ଡ ଠାକୁର ॥

Karapatra joḍiṇa muṁ boili uttara | Sābadhāna hoi śuṇa brahmāṇḍa ṭhākura ||

With folded hands, I give you this reply (or answer). | Listen attentively, O Lord of the Universe.

ଅଷ୍ଟଦିନେ ପଡ଼ିବ ମୋହର ଗୁରୁବାର । ପଡ଼ି ଚରଚିବି ମୁହିଁ ସଭିଙ୍କର ଘର ॥

Aṣṭadine padiba mohar gurubāra | Padi caracibi muhin sabhiṅkara ghara ||

In eight days will come my Thursday (day of Lakshmi vrata observance). | On that day, I shall go house to house.

ପଡ଼ି ଚରଚିବି କୀଟୁ ବ୍ରହ୍ମ ପରିଯନ୍ତେ । ଏହି ଦୋଷ ମୋର ପ୍ରଭୁ ନ ଧରିବ ଚିତ୍ତେ ॥

Padi caracibi kīṭu brahma parijante | Ehi doṣa mora prabhu na dhariba citte ||

I shall visit houses — from insects (smallest beings) up to Brahma (the creator). | O Lord, may you not keep this fault of minc in your heart.

ହେଉ ବୋଲି ଶ୍ରୀମୁଖରେ ଆଜ୍ଞା ଅଛ ଦେଇ । ଏବେ କିମ୍ପା ସତ୍ୟ ଭଗ୍ନ ହେଉଛ ଗୋସାଇଁ ॥

Heu boli śrīmukhare ājñā achha dei | Ebe kimpā satya bhagna heucha gosāin ||

Saying "let it be so," you had given your command from your revered mouth. | Now, Lord, are you going to break that sacred truth (your own word)?

ଜଗନ୍ନାଥ କହୁଛନ୍ତି କୋପଭର ହୋଇ । ବାପ ତୋ ଲୁଣିଆ ଯେ ଗରଜି ମରୁଥାଇ ॥

Jagannātha kahuchanti kōpabhara hoi | Bāpa to luṇiā je garaji maruthāi ||

Jagannath speaks, filled with anger: | "Your father, the salt merchant, shouts (thunders) and dies in rage (used in a derogatory or low-status context)!"

ଝିଅଟେରୀ ତୋ ଦୁର୍ଗୁଣ କହିଲେ ନ ସରେ | ବାପର ଗର୍ଜ୍ଜନ ଶବ୍ଦେ କିଏ ରହିପାରେ ॥

Jhiāṭerī to durguṇa kahile na sare | Bāpara garjjana śabde ki'e rahipāre ||

"You are merely a squint-eyed girl — just naming your faults won't suffice!" | "Who can stand before the thunderous voice of your father?"

ଚାରିପାଖେ ମେଘନାଦ ପାଚେରୀ ତୋଳାଇ । ବଡ଼ ଦେଉଳରେ ରହିଅଛୁ ଦୁଇଭାଇ ॥

Cāripākhe meghanāda pācerī toḷāi | Baḍa deūḷare rahi'achu duibhāi ||

Thunder roars all around, raising curtains (the temple is surrounded by a boundary wall called 'Meghanada'). | In the grand temple, we are staying, the two brothers (Jagannath and Balabhadra).

ମହାଲକ୍ଷ୍ମୀ ବୋଲୁଛନ୍ତି ଠାକୁରଙ୍କୁ ଚାହିଁ । ଅଛବର ଘରେ ଦଣ୍ଡେ ଥିଲି ଉଭାହୋଇ ॥

Mahālakṣmī boluchanti ṭhākuraṅku cāhin | Acchabara ghare daṇḍe thili ubhāhoi ||

Mahalakshmi speaks while looking at the Lord (Jagannath): | "I was standing upright in Achhaba's house,"

ଅଛବ ବିଟାଳ ବୋଲି ଦିଅ ଘଉଡ଼ାଇ । ପୁଣି ଜାତି କୁଳ ଗୋତ୍ର କହିଲ ଗୋସାଇଁ ॥

Acchaba biṭāḷa boli di'a gha'uḍāi | Puṇi jāti kuḷa gotra kahila gosāin ||

"Calling Achhaba a 'Bitala' (low-born or unclean), you expelled me (gave me exile)." | "Again, O Lord, you mentioned caste, family, and lineage."

ପ୍ରଭୁ ହେତୁ ସବୁ ଯାଉଅଛି ଗୋପ୍ୟ ହୋଇ । ତୁମ ଜାତି କୁଳର ତ ଠିକଣା ନ ଥାଇ ॥

Prabhu hetu sabu jāu'achi gopya hoi | Tuma jāti kuḷara ta ṭhikāṇā na thāi ||

"For the sake of the Lord, all things (such distinctions) become secret or hidden." | "There is no definite identity for your caste and family background."

ତୁମ ଜାତି କୁଳ ଯେ କହିଲେ ନ ସରଇ । ଗଉଡ଼ ଘରେ ରହିଲ ଦୁଇଗୋଟି ଭାଇ ॥

Tuma jāti kuḷa je kahile na sarai | Gauḍa ghare rahila duigoṭi bhāi ||

"If someone tries to speak of your caste or lineage, it cannot be established." | "You two brothers stayed in a Gauda (lower-caste) household."

ନିମା ନାମେ ସିପୁଟି ଯେ ଜାତିରେ ଗୋଲକ । ତାହାଘରେ ଜଗନ୍ନାଥ କଲ ଅନ୍ନଭକ୍ଷ୍ ॥

Nimā nāme sipuṭi je jātire golaka | Tāhāghare jagannātha kala annabhakṣa ||

"A woman named Nima from the Siputi caste (a potter or artisan community), of the Golaka clan," | "It was in her house that Jagannath ate cooked food (rice/meal)."

ଦୂତ ପଣେ ଯାଇଥିଲ ହସ୍ତିନା ଭୁବନ | ବିଦୁର ଘରେ ଯେ ପୁଣି କରିଲ ଭୋଜନ ॥

Druta paṇe jāithila hastinā bhubana | Bidura ghare je puṇi karila bhojana ||

"You swiftly went to Hastinapur (the city of elephants – capital of the Kauravas)." | "And there, again, you ate food in the house of Vidura."

ଜାରାନାମେ ଶବର ଯେ ଅରଣ୍ୟରେ ଘର । ସେ ତୁମ୍ଭଙ୍କୁ ପୂଜିଲା ବରଷ ଦଶବାର ॥

Jārānāme śabara je araṇyare ghara | Se tumbhaṅku pūjilā baraṣa daśavāra ||

"A hunter named Jara, who had a house in the forest," | "He worshipped you ten times a year (or for ten years)."

ଅରଣ୍ୟର ଫଳମୂଳ ଖୋଜିଣ ଆଣଇ । ବସିଣ ପ୍ରଥମେ ଭଲମନ୍ଦ ସେ ଖାଅଇ ॥

Araṇyara phaḷamūla khojiṇa āṇai | Basiṇa prathame bhalamanda se khā'ai ||

"He searched the forest for fruits and roots and brought them." | "He sat and first tasted each to check if they were good or bad."

ପିତା କଷା ସବୁ ପ୍ରଭୁ ଆଡ଼ କରିଦେଇ । ଯେ ଫଳ ସୁଆଦ ତାହା ତୁମ୍ଭଙ୍କୁ ଭୁଞ୍ଜାଇ ॥

Pitā kaṣā sabu prabhu āda karidei | Je phaḷa suāda tāhā tumbhaṅku bhuñjā'i ||

"He spat out the sour or bitter ones and set them aside, O Lord." | "And whatever fruits were tasty; he fed them to you."

ଶବର ବିଟାଳ ତୁମ୍ଭେ ବେନିଗୋଟି ଭାଇ | ଏକଥା କି ତୁମ୍ଭ ମନୁ ଗଲା ଭୁଲି ହୋଇ ॥

Śabara biṭāḷa tumbhe benigoṭi bhāi | Ekathā ki tumbha manu galā bhuli hoi ||

"You (two) brothers are also of the Shabara (tribal) lineage." | "Have you forgotten this fact from your minds in delusion?"

ଆପଣେ ପାତକୀ କିମ୍ପା ପରନିନ୍ଦା କର | ପାପ ପୁଣ୍ୟ ଦୁଇ କଥା ବିଚାର ନ କର ॥

Āpaṇe pātakī kimpā paraniñdā kara | Pāpa puṇya dui kathā bicāra na kara ||

"Whether you yourself are a sinner or speak ill of others," | "You make no judgment between sin and virtue."

ଭାରିଯା ଯେ ଦୋଷକଲେ ପତି ତା ସହଇ | ଏକ ଅପରାଧ ପ୍ରଭୁ ଭୃତ୍ୟେ କି ତେଜଇ ॥

Bhārijā je doṣakale pati tā sahai | Eka aparādha prabhu bhṛutye ki tejai ||

"If the wife (Bhariya) commits a fault, the husband shares in it." | "Does a master abandon his servant for a single mistake?"

କିମ୍ପା ନକର ଗୋସାଇଁ ଏମନ୍ତ ବିଚାର । ଯାଅ ଯାଅ ବୋଲୁଅଛ ମୋତେ ବାରମ୍ବାର ॥

Kimpā nakara gosāin emanta bicāra | Jā'a jā'a bolu'acha mote bārambāra ||

"Oh Lord, please don't make such a judgment." | "You keep telling me 'Go, leave' again and again."

ଜଗନ୍ନାଥ କହୁଅଛି ଏମନ୍ତ କରିବା | ମାଣେ ମାଣେ ପଡ଼ି ତୋତେ ନିତ୍ୟେ ଦେଉଥିବା ॥

Jagannātha kahu'achi emanta karibā | Māṇe māṇe padi tote nitye de'uthibā ||

Jagannath says: "Let's do one thing, | I keep yielding to your wishes day by day, honouring your pride."

ଭାଇଙ୍କୁ ବୁଝାଇ ପଛେ ତୁମ୍ଭଙ୍କୁ ଆଣିବୁ । ଭାଇଙ୍କ ଆଜ୍ଞା ଅବଜ୍ଞା କେଭେ ନ କରିବୁ ॥

Bhāiṅku bujhā'i pacche tumbhaṅku āṇibu | Bhāiṅka ājñā abajñā kebhe na karibu ll

I will bring you back after convincing my elder brother. | Never should I disobey my elder brother's command.

ଲକ୍ଷ୍ମୀଦେବୀ କହନ୍ତି ପଡ଼ିରେ କାର୍ଯ୍ୟ ନାହିଁ । ଅନାଥ ଅରକ୍ଷ ପ୍ରାୟ ଯାଉଅଛି ମୁହିଁ ॥

Lakṣmīdevī kahanti padire kārya nāhin | Anātha arakṣa prāya jāu'achi muhin ll

Lakshmi Devi says: There is no purpose in staying here anymore. | I am going away like one who is abandoned and unprotected.

ରାଣ୍ଡୀ ଅଲକ୍ଷଣୀ ଝିଅ ମୁହିଁ ଯେ ନୁହଇ । ପିତାର ଘରକୁ ମୁଁ ଯେ ବାହାରି ଯିବଇଁ ॥

Rāṇḍī alakṣaṇī jhiā muhin je nuha'i | Pitāra gharaku mun je bāhāri jibain ll

I am not an inauspicious widow or unfortunate girl. | I will return to my father's home.

ତୁମ୍ଭ ଅଳଙ୍କାର ମାନ ପ୍ରଭୁ କାଢ଼ି ନିଅ । ପଛରେ ମୋତେ ଯେ ଆଉ ବୋଲଣା ନ ଦିଅ ॥

Tuma alaṅkāra māna prabhu kāḍhi nia | Pacchare mote je ā'u bolaṇā na dia ll

O Lord, take back the ornaments you have given me. | Hereafter, from behind, you no longer even speak to me about this.

ଗୋବିନ୍ଦ ବୋଲନ୍ତି ଲକ୍ଷ୍ମୀ ହୋଇଲୁକି ବାଇ । ଅଙ୍ଗ ଅଳଙ୍କାର ଆମ୍ଭେ ନେବୁ କାହିଁ ପାଇଁ ॥

Govinda bolanti Lakṣmī hoiluki bā'ī | Aṅga alaṅkāra āmbhe nebu kāhin pāin ll

Govinda (Lord Jagannath) says:" Are you out of your mind? | Why should we take back the ornaments worn on your body?"

ଭାରିଜା ଦେହରେ ଯେଉଁ ଅଳଙ୍କାର ଥାଏ । ସ୍ୱାମୀହୋଇ ତାହାଠାରୁ କାଢ଼ିଣ କି ନିଏ ॥

Bhārijā dehare jeun alaṅkāra thā'e | Svāmīhoi tāhāṭhāru kāḍhiṇa ki nie ll

The ornaments that are on the wife's body | Can a husband forcibly remove those ornaments from her?

ଠାକୁରାଣୀ କହୁଛନ୍ତି ଶ୍ରୀମୁଖକୁ ଚାହିଁ । ତୁମ୍ଭର ଅଟଇ ମୁଁ ଯେ ପ୍ରଥମ ବିବାହୀ ॥

Ṭhakurāṇī kahuchanti śrīmukhaku cāhin | Tumbhara aṭa'i mun je prathama bibāhī ||

The Goddess (Lakshmi) speaks, looking at the Lord's divine face: | I am your lawful (eldest) first wife.

ପଛିରେ କହିବ ଲକ୍ଷ୍ମୀ ଆମ ଘରେ ଥିଲା । ସହସ୍ର ଟଙ୍କାର ଅଳଙ୍କାର ଘେନିଗଲା ॥

Pacchire kahiba Lakṣmī āma ghare thilā | Sahasra ṭaṅkāra alaṅkāra ghenigalā ||

Later You will say: Lakshmi was once in our house, | ...and she took away ornaments worth thousands of coins.

ଏମନ୍ତ ଅଖ୍ୟାତି ମୋତେ ନଦିଅ ଗୋସାଇଁ । ତୁମ୍ଭ ଅଳଙ୍କାର ମାନ ନିଅ ବାହୁଡ଼ାଇ ॥

Emanta akhyāti mote nadi'a gosāin | Tumbha alaṅkāra māna nia bāhudā'i ||

O Lord, do not give me such a bad reputation. | Take back all your ornaments and honour—return them respectfully.

ଶିରରୁ କାଢ଼ିଲେ ଲକ୍ଷ ମୁକୁତାର ଜାଲି । ହୃଦରୁ କାଢ଼ିଲେ ଇନ୍ଦ୍ର ଗୋବିନ୍ଦ କଞ୍ଚୁଲି ॥

Śiraru kāḍhile lakṣa mukutāra jāli | Hṛudaru kāḍhile indra govinda kañculi ll

From her head, she removed the netted crown made of lakhs of pearls. | From her chest, she took off the divine bodice of Indra and Govinda (symbolizing great richness or divinity).

ଅଣ୍ଟାରୁ କାଢ଼ିଲେ ମାଏ ରତ୍ନ ଓଢ଼ିଆଣୀ । ନାସିକାରୁ କାଢ଼ିଲେ ଯେ ମୁକୁତା ବସଣୀ ॥

Aṇṭāru kāḍhile mā'e ratna oḍhiāṇī | Nāsikāru kāḍhile je mukutā basaṇī ll

From her waist, the mother removed the jewel-embroidered waist-sash. | From her nose, she removed the pearl nose-ring.

କର୍ଣ୍ଣ ଦ୍ୱୟରୁ କାଢ଼ିଲେ ହୀରାର କୁଣ୍ଡଳ । ଗଳାରୁ କାଢ଼ିଲେ ଯେ ଦୋସରୀ ଚିନାମାଳ ॥

Karṇa dyayaru kāḍhile hīrāra kuṇḍala | Gaḷāru kāḍhile je dosarī chināmāḷa ll

From both ears, she took off the diamond earrings. | From her neck, she removed the second necklace made of Chinese pearls (or a necklace of distinctive gems).

ପାଦରୁ କାଢ଼ିଲେ ଦେବୀ ବାଜେଣୀ ନୁପୂର । ଅଙ୍ଗୁଷ୍ଠିରୁ କାଢ଼ିଲେ ଯେ ଝୁଣ୍ଟିଆ ସତ୍ୱର ॥

Pādarū kāḍhile Devī bājeṇī nupūra | Aṅguṣṭhiru kāḍhile je jhuṇṭiā satvara ||

From her feet, the goddess removed the musical anklets (nūpur). | From her toes, she removed the dangling toe-rings or ornaments instantly.

ଅନ୍ୟ ଅଳଙ୍କାରମାନ କି କହିବି ଆଉ । ରୁଣ୍ଡ କଲାରୁ ଦିଶିଲା ସବୁ ଦାଉ ଦାଉ ॥

Anya alaṅkāramāna ki kahibi ā'u | Ruṇḍa kalāru diśilā sabu dā'u dā'u ||

What more can I say about the other ornaments? | When gathered together, all the ornaments glittered visibly.

ସବୁ ଅଳଙ୍କାରମାନ ଏକଠାବ କଲେ । ରଖ ଦୀନବନ୍ଧୁ ଏହାବୋଲି ସମର୍ପିଲେ ॥

Sabu alaṅkāramāna ekaṭhāba kale | Rakha dīnabandhu ehāboli samarpile ||

She gathered all her ornaments together. | Saying "Keep this, O protector of the poor," she offered them (to Him).

ଗୋବିନ୍ଦ କହନ୍ତି ଏହା କି କରିବୁ ନେଇ । ଆମ୍ଭର ଏ ଅଳଙ୍କାରେ ପ୍ରୟୋଜନ ନାହିଁ ॥

Govinda kahanti ehā ki karibu nei | Āmbhara e alaṅkāre prayojana nāhin ll

Govinda said, "What will I do by taking this?" | We have no use for these ornaments.

ଗୃହସ୍ଥ ହୋଇଣ ଯେବେ ଭାର୍ଯ୍ୟାକୁ ତେଜଇ । ଛ' ମାସକୁ ଭାତ ଲୁଗା ଲେଖିଣ ଦିଅଇ ॥

Gṛuhastha ho'iṇ jebe bhāryāku tejai | Cha' māsaku bhāta lugā lekhiṇa di'āi ll

When a householder disowns his wife, | He must provide her rice and cloth for six months in writing (i.e., as legal obligation).

ଏହି ଅଳଙ୍କାର ସବୁ ତୁମ୍ଭେ ଘେନିଯାଅ | ବିକି ଭାଙ୍ଗିକରି ଭାତ ଲୁଗା କରୁଥାଅ ॥

Ehi alaṅkāra sabu tumbhe ghenijā'a | Biki bhāṅkikari bhāta lugā karuthā'a ll

You take away all these ornaments. | Sell and break them to arrange food and clothing (for Her).

ଲକ୍ଷ୍ମୀଦେବୀ କହୁଛନ୍ତି ପ୍ରଭୁ ମୁଖ ଚାହିଁ | ସାବଧାନ ହୋଇ ଶୁଣ ବ୍ରହ୍ମାଣ୍ଡ ଗୋସାଇଁ ||

Lakṣmīdevī kahuchanti prabhu mukha cāhin | Sābadhāna hoi śuṇa brahmāṇḍa gosāin ||

Goddess Lakshmi speaks, looking at the Lord's face: | Listen carefully, O Lord of the universe.

ମୋର ତୁଲେ ଆଉ ଯେଉଁ ଭାରିଯା ଆଣିବ | ଏହିସବୁ ଅଳଙ୍କାର ତାହାଙ୍କୁ ଯେ ଦେବ ||

Mora tule ā'u jeun bhārijā āṇiba | Ehisabu alaṅkāra tāhāṅku je deba ||

If you bring another wife in place of me, | Then give all these ornaments to her.

ମୁହିଁ ଯାଉଅଛି ହୀନ ଅରକ୍ଷିତ ହୋଇ | ମୋହ ଅଭିଶାପ ଘେନ ପ୍ରଭୁ ଭାବଗ୍ରାହୀ ||

Muhin jāu'achi hīna arakṣita hoi | Moha abhiśāpa ghena prabhu bhābagrāhī ||

I am going away, weak and unprotected, | O compassionate Lord, take this curse of my sorrow (with You).

ସତେ ଯେବେ ଚନ୍ଦ୍ର ସୂର୍ଯ୍ୟ ହୋନ୍ତି ଆତଯାତ । ତୁମ୍ଭଙ୍କୁ ଅନ୍ନ ନ ମିଳୁ ଆହେ ଜଗନ୍ନାଥ ॥

Sate jebe candra sūrya honti ātajāta | Tumbhaṅku anna na miḷu āhe jagannātha ll

Truly, when the Moon and Sun reverse their courses, | May you not receive food, O Jagannath.

ବାରବର୍ଷ ଯାଏ ତୁମ୍ଭେ ଦରିଦ୍ର ହୋଇବ । ଅନ୍ନ ବସ୍ତ୍ର ଜଳ ଯେ ତୁମ୍ଭଙ୍କୁ ନ ମିଳିବ ॥

Bārabarṣa jāe tumbhe daridra hoiba | Anna bastra jaḷa je tumbhaṅku na miḷiba ll

For twelve years you shall live in poverty, | And may you not get food, clothes, or water.

ମୁହିଁ ଚଣ୍ଡାଳୁଣୀ ଯେବେ ଟେକିଦେବି ଅନ୍ନ । ଭୋଜନ କରିବେ ତେବେ କାଳୀୟ ଗଞ୍ଜନ ॥

Muhin caṇḍāluṇī jebe ṭekidebi anna | Bhojana karibe tebe kāḷīya gañjana ll

When I, a Chandāla woman, will offer (serve) food, | Only then will the Kaliya (Lord) consume food.

ଏତେ ବୋଲି ଲକ୍ଷ୍ମୀ ଦେବୀ ଶାପ ଦେଇ ଗଲେ ।ଦେଉଳୁ ବାହାର ହୋଇ କେତେଦୂର ଗଲେ ॥

Ete boli Lakṣmī Devī śāpa dei gale | Deuḷu bāhāra hoi kete dūra gale ll

Saying this, Goddess Lakshmi gave a curse and left. | She exited the temple and went some distance away.

ଏହାଦେଖି ଦାସୀମାନେ ସଙ୍ଗେ ଗୋଡ଼ାଅନ୍ତି ।ଦାସୀଙ୍କୁ ଅନାଇ ଲକ୍ଷ୍ମୀଦେବୀ ବୋଲୁଛନ୍ତି ॥

Ehādekhi dāsīmāne saṅge goḍānti | Dāsīṅku anā'i Lakṣmīdevī boluchanti ll

Seeing this, the maidservants started following her. | Looking at the maidservants, Goddess Lakshmi says:

ମୁହିଁ ଯାଉଅଛି ହୀନ ଅଲକ୍ଷଣୀ ହୋଇ । ମୋର ପଛେ ତୁମ୍ଭେମାନେ ଆସୁଛ କିମ୍ପାଇଁ ॥

Muhiṁ jāu'achi hīna alakṣaṇī hoi | Mora pacche tumbhemāne āsucha kimpāin ll

I am going, now unfortunate and inauspicious. | Why are you all coming behind me?

ଏହିପରି ହୋଇ ଯେବେ ପିତାଘର ଯିବି । ଚାରିଦିନ ମାତ୍ର ତହିଁ ରହି ନ ପାରିବି ॥

Ehipari hoi jebe pitāghara jibi | Cāridina mātra tahin rahi na pāribi ll

In this condition, when I go to my father's house, | I will not be able to stay there even for four days.

ଜଗନ୍ନାଥ ପ୍ରାୟବନ୍ଧୁ ପିତାଘର ଯିବେ । ତାଙ୍କୁ ଦେଖି ପିତା ମୋତେ ସମର୍ପିଣ ଦେବେ ॥

Jagannātha prāyabandhu pitāghara jibe | Tāṅku dekhi pitā mote samarpīṇa debe ll

Jagannath, the beloved, will come to the in-laws' house (my father's house). | Seeing him, my father will hand me over to him again.

ଶାପ ଦେବା ଫଳ ମୋ ହୋଇବ ଅକାରଣ । ଦରିଦ୍ର ନୋହିବେ ପ୍ରଭୁ ଦେବ ଭଗବାନ ॥

Śāpa debā phaḷa mo hoiba akāraṇa | Daridra nohibe prabhu deba bhagabāna ll

The result of giving the curse will be pointless for me. | The Lord (Jagannath) will not become poor.

ଏତେ ବୋଲି ଲକ୍ଷ୍ମୀଦେବୀ ମନେ ଚିନ୍ତାକଲେ । ବିଶ୍ୱକର୍ମାଙ୍କୁ ଯେ ମାଏ ମନେ ସୁମରିଲେ ॥

Ete boli Lakṣmīdevī mane cintākale | Biśvakarmāku je mā'e mane sumarile ll

Saying this, Goddess Lakshmi thought in her mind. | She mentally remembered Lord Vishwakarma (the celestial architect).

ବୈକୁଣ୍ଠପୁରରେ ବିଶ୍ୱକର୍ମା ରହିଥିଲା । ସ୍ମରଣ ମାତ୍ରକେ ଲକ୍ଷ୍ମୀ ଛାମୁରେ ମିଳିଲା ॥

Vaikunṭhapurare Biśvakarmā rahithilā | Smaraṇa mātrake Lakṣmī chāmure miḷilā ll

Vishwakarma was residing in Vaikunthapur (Vaikuntha, celestial abode). | Just upon remembrance, he appeared immediately before Lakshmi.

କିସ ଆଜ୍ଞା ହେଉ ମୋତେ ଲକ୍ଷ୍ମୀ ମହାମାୟୀ । ଶୁଣି ଆଜ୍ଞାଦେଲେ ବିଶ୍ୱକର୍ମାଙ୍କୁ ଯେ ଚାହିଁ ॥

Kisa ājñā he'u mote Lakṣmī mahāmāyī | Śuṇi ājñādele Biśvakarmaku je cāhın ll

What is your command for me, O Lakshmi, the great illusionary Goddess? | Hearing this, She gave instructions to Vishwakarma, looking at him.

ଚଣ୍ଡାଲୁଣୀ ଅପବାଦେ ପ୍ରଭୁ ଦେଲେ ଘଉଡ଼ାଇ । ପାରିବୁକି ଖଣ୍ଡିଏ କୁଡ଼ିଆ ତୋଳିଦେଇ ॥

Caṇḍāluṇī apabāde prabhu dele ghaudā'i | Pāribuki khaṇḍie kudiā toḷide'i ll

Calling me as Chandāluṇī (outcaste woman), the Lord has expelled me. | Can you build a thatched hut for me?

ଆଜ୍ଞାମାତ୍ରେ ବିଶ୍ୱକର୍ମା ବେଗେ ଚଳିଗଲେ । ତିନିକୋଶ ପ୍ରମାଣେ ଉଆସ ତୋଳାଇଲେ ॥

Ājñāmātre Biśvakarmā bege caligale | Tinikośa pramāṇe uāsa toḷāile ll

At just the order, Vishwakarma immediately went on his way. | He raised a palace (mansion) extending three kosas (a kosa is a traditional unit of distance).

ସୁବର୍ଣ୍ଣର କାନ୍ଥମାନ ସବୁଘରେ କଲେ । ହୀରା ନୀଳା ମାଣିକ୍ୟାଦି ତହିଁ ଖଞ୍ଜାଇଲେ ॥

Subarṇara kānthamāna sabughare kale | Hīrā nīlā māṇikyādi tahin khañjāile ll

He made all the walls of the houses out of gold. | There he inlaid diamonds, sapphires, rubies, and other gems.

ଗଣ୍ଠିସ୍ଥଳେ ଅନେକ ମୁକୁତା ଲଗାଇଲେ । ପ୍ରବାଳର ସ୍ତମ୍ଭମାନ ତହିଁରେ ରଚିଲେ ॥

Gaṇṭhisthale aneka mukutā lagāile | Prabāḷara stambhamāna tahinre racile ll

He adorned the corners of the structure with many pearls. | There he constructed pillars made of coral.

ପୁର ଦେଖି କମଳିନୀ ସନ୍ତୁଷ୍ଟ ହୋଇଲେ । ବିଶ୍ୱକର୍ମାକୁ ବହୁତ ପ୍ରଶଂସା ଯେ କଲେ ॥

Pura dekhi kamalinī santuṣṭa hoile | Biśvakarmāku bahuta praśansā je kale ll

Seeing the palace, Kamalini (Goddess Lakshmi) became pleased. | She greatly praised Vishwakarma.

ବୈକୁଣ୍ଠ ପୁରକୁ ବିଶ୍ୱକର୍ମା ଚଳିଗଲେ । ଅଷ୍ଟବେତାଳକୁ ଡାକି ଦେବୀ ଆଜ୍ଞା ଦେଲେ ॥

Vaikuntha puraku Viśvakarmā caligale | Aṣṭabetāḷaku ḍāki Devī ājñā dele ll

Vishwakarma departed for Vaikuntha city. | The Goddess called the eight spirits (Aṣṭa Vetāla) and gave them instructions.

ଅଷ୍ଟ ବେତାଳରେ ତୁମ୍ଭେ ଏମନ୍ତ କରିବ । ପ୍ରଥମେ ରୋଷାଇ ଶାଳେ ଯାଇଣ ପଶିବ ॥

Aṣṭa betāḷare tumbhe emanta kariba | Prathame roṣā'i śāḷe jāiṇa paśiba ll

You eight Vetālas will do this task. | First, you will go and enter the kitchen hall.

ଷାଠିଏ ପଉଟି ଭୋଗ ଭୁଞ୍ଜିବ ଯେ ତହିଁ । ତେରପୌଟି ବ୍ୟଞ୍ଜନ ଖାଇବ ହର୍ଷହୋଇ ॥

Ṣāṭhi'e pauṭi bhōga bhuñjiba je tahin | Terapauṭi vyañjana khāiba harṣaho'i ll

There, you shall eat sixty types of food offerings. | And joyfully eat thirteen varieties of delicacies.

ଶାଗମୁଗ ମଧୁରୁଚି ତିକ୍ତ କାଞ୍ଜିରାଇ । ଆମ୍ବିଳ ଖାଇବ ଖଣ୍ଡାଶାକର ମିଶାଇ ॥

Śāgamuga madhuruci tikta kāñjirā'i | Āmbiḷa khāiba khaṇḍāśākara misā'i ll

Spinach and moong (green gram), sweet-tasting and slightly bitter fermented soup (kanjirāi). | Then you will eat sour curry (ambila) mixed with khanda leafy greens.

ଅମୃତ ମଣୋହୀ ମାନ ଭୋଜନ କରିବ । ହାଣ୍ଡିମାନ ନେଇ ଏକଠାବେ କଚାଡ଼ିବ ॥

Amṛuta maṇohī māna bhojana kariba | Hāṇḍimāna nei ekaṭhābe kacāḍiba ||

You will eat divine, delightful food. | Then gather all the pots and break them together in one place.

ତହୁଁ ଯାଇଣ ଭଣ୍ଡାର ମଧ୍ୟରେ ପଶିବ । ବାଉନକୋଟି ଭଣ୍ଡାର ବୋହିଣ ଆଣିବ ॥

Tahun jāiṇa bhaṇḍāra madhyare paśiba | Bā'unakoṭi bhaṇḍāra bohina āṇiba ||

Then you will go and enter the storeroom. | Bring the store items of the fifty-two crores' warehouse.

କାଣି କଉଡ଼ି କଡ଼ାକର ଦ୍ରବ୍ୟ ନ ରଖିବ । ସବୁ ବୋହି ଆଣି ମୋର ପାଶେ ସମର୍ପିବ ॥

Kāṇi ka'udi kaḍākara dravya na rakhiba | Sabu bohi āṇi mora pāśe samarpiba ||

Do not leave behind a single cowrie or coin of value. | Bring and offer everything at my (Lakshmi's) feet.

ବେତାଳ ବୋଇଲେ ମହାଲକ୍ଷ୍ମୀ ମୁଖ ଚାହିଁ । କେମନ୍ତ କରିଣ ତହୁଁ ଆଣିବୁ ବୁହାଇ ॥

Betāḷa boile mahālakṣmī mukha cāhin | Kementa kariṇa tahun āṇibu buhā'i ll

The Vetalas said, looking at Mahalakshmi's face, | How can we carry and bring those things from there?

ଜଗନ୍ନାଥ ମହାପ୍ରଭୁ ତହିଁ ଚେଇଁଥିବେ । ଆମ୍ଭଙ୍କୁ ଦେଖିଣ କାଳେ ପରାଭବ ଦେବେ ॥

Jagannātha mahāprabhu tahin ce'inthibe | Āmbhaṅku dekhiṇa kāḷe parābhaba debe ll

Lord Jagannath will be watching over there. | If He sees us, He will defeat us or curse us.

ଶୁଣି କମଳିନୀ ନିଦ୍ରାବତୀକି ରାଇଲେ । ବହନ ମୋ ବୋଲକର ବୋଲିଣ ବୋଇଲେ ॥

Śuṇi kamalinī nidrābatīki rāile | Bahana mo bolakara boliṇa boile ll

Hearing this, Kamalini (Lakshmi) started remembering Nidrābati (the Goddess of sleep). | She said, "My carriers, you follow my word."

ରାମକୃଷ୍ଣ ନୟନରେ ନିଦ୍ରା ଯେ ଘାରିବୁ । କାଲି ବେଳ ଦୁଇଘଡ଼ି ଯାଏ ନ ଛାଡ଼ିବୁ ॥

Rāmakṛuṣṇa nayanare nidrā je ghāribu | Kāli beḷa duighadi jāe na chāḍibu ll

Sprinkle sleep in the eyes of Ramakrishna. | Until tomorrow till two in the afternoon, do not release (the sleep).

ଆଜ୍ଞାପାଇ ନିଦ୍ରାବତୀ ଶୀଘ୍ର ଚଳିଗଲେ । ରାମକୃଷ୍ଣ ନୟନରେ ନିଦ୍ରା ଯେ ଘାରିଲେ ॥

Ājñāpā'i nidrābatī śīghra caligale | Rāmakṛuṣṇa nayanare nidrā je ghārile ll

Upon receiving the command, Nidrabati (the Goddess of sleep) quickly went. | She sprinkled sleep into the eyes of Ramakrishna.

ପାକଶାଳାରେ ବେତାଳ ପ୍ରବେଶ ହୋଇଲେ । ତହିଁ ଥିବା ପାକଦ୍ରବ୍ୟ ସମସ୍ତ ଖାଇଲେ ॥

Pākśāḷāre betāḷa prabeśa hoile | Tahin thibā pākadrabya samasta khāile ll

The Vetalas entered the kitchen. | They ate all the cooked items that were there.

ହାଣ୍ଡିମାନ ସବୁ ଏକଠାବେ କଚାଡ଼ିଲେ । ଭଣ୍ଡାର ଘରରେ ଅଷ୍ଟବେତାଳ ପଶିଲେ ॥

Hāṇḍimāna sabu ekaṭhābe kacāḍile | Bhaṇḍāra gharare aṣṭabetāḷa paśile ll

They gathered and clanged together all the cooking pots. | The eight Vetalas entered the storeroom.

ଯେତେ ଦ୍ରବ୍ୟ ପୂର୍ଣ୍ଣ ହୋଇ ରହିଥିଲା ତହିଁ । ବାଉନକୋଟି ଭଣ୍ଡାର ଆଣିଲେ ବୁହାଇ ॥

Jete drabya pūrṇa ho'i rahithilā tahin | Bā'unakoṭi bhaṇḍāra āṇile buhā'i ll

As much wealth/materials as were completely stored there, | The fifty-two crore storehouses were emptied and carried away stealthily.

ରାତ୍ର ଷୋଳ ଘଡ଼ିଯାକ ବେତାଳ ଯେ ତହିଁ | କୁଲାରୁ ଛାଞ୍ଚୁଣିଯାକ ସବୁ ନେଲେ ବୋହି ॥

Rātra ṣoḷa ghadijāka betāḷa je tahin | Kulāru chāñchuṇijāka sabu nele bohi ll

For sixteen hours of the night, the Vetalas were there, | From baskets to sieves — they took and carried away everything.

ଦେଖିକରି ମହାଲକ୍ଷ୍ମୀ ସନ୍ତୁଷ୍ଟ ହୋଇଲେ । ତୁମ୍ଭେ ଆଜି ପୁତ୍ରପଣ କରିଲ ବୋଇଲେ ॥

Dekhikari Mahālakṣmī santuṣṭa hoile | Tumbhe āji putrapaṇa karila boile ll

Seeing this, Mahalakshmi was pleased. | She said, "Today you have acted like true sons (faithful servants)."

ପ୍ରଶଂସା କରିଣ ମାଏ ବଚନ ଯେ କହି । ସବୁ ଦ୍ରବ୍ୟ ଆଣିଲ ତ ରତ୍ନଖଟ ନାହିଁ ॥

Praśansā kariṇa mā'e bacana je kahi | Sabu drabya āṇila ta ratnakhata nāhin ll

The mother (Lakshmi) praised them and then spoke these words, | You brought all the wealth, but the gem-studded cot is missing.

ପାଞ୍ଚଲକ୍ଷ ମୂଲ୍ୟ ସେହି ଖଟତ ଅଟଇ । ଯାଅରେ ବେତାଳ ଏବେ ଖଟ ଆଣ ବୋହି ॥

Pāñcalakṣa mūlya sehi khaṭata aṭa'i | Jā'are betāḷa ebe khaṭa āṇa bohi ll

That cot alone is worth five lakh (coins/units of currency). | Go now, Vetala, and bring the cot carrying it here.

ଯେତେବେଳେ ଜଗନ୍ନାଥ ଦରିଦ୍ର ହୋଇବେ । ରତ୍ନ ଖଟ ବିକି କରି ଦିନ ଚଳାଇବେ ॥

Jetebeḷe Jagannātha daridra hoibe | Ratna khaṭa biki kari dina calāibe ll

Whenever Lord Jagannath becomes poor, | They will sell the gem cot and manage the offerings/charities.

ଯେବେ ଜଗନ୍ନାଥପ୍ରଭୁ ମୋତେ ନ ଖୋଜିବେ । ନାରୀଙ୍କୁ ପୁରୁଷମାନେ ଆଉ ନ ଲୋଡ଼ିବେ ॥

Jebe Jagannāthaprabhu mote na khojibe | Nāriṅku puruṣamāne ā'u na lodibe ll

When Lord Jagannath will no longer search for me, | Men will no longer desire or chase after women.

ମୋତେ ଘେନି ପ୍ରଭୁ ଯେବେ ନ କରିବେ ଘର । କଳିଯୁଗେ ନାରୀଙ୍କି ଯେ ନ ଖୋଜିବେ ନର ॥

Mote ghēni prabhu jebe na karibe ghara | Kaḷiyuge nāriṅka je na khojibe nara ll

When the Lord no longer takes me back into His home, | In the age of Kali, men will no longer seek women.

ବେତାଳେ ବୋଲୁଅଛନ୍ତି ରମା ମୁଖ ଚାହିଁ । ରତ୍ନଖଟେ ଶୋଇଛନ୍ତି ଦୁଇଗୋଟି ଭାଇ ॥

Betāḷe bolu'achanti ramā mukha cāhin | Ratnakhate sho'ichanti duigoṭi bhā'i ll

Vetala(s) are speaking while looking at the face of Rama (Lakshmi). | On the gem-studded cot, the two brothers are lying (asleep).

କୋଟିସିଂହ ପରାକ୍ରମ ପ୍ରଭୁ ବଳରାମ । ପୁଣି ତହିଁ ଶୋଇଛନ୍ତି କାଳୀୟ ଗଞ୍ଜନ ॥

Koṭisiṁha parākrama prabhu baḷarāma | Puṇi tahin sho'ichanti kāḷīya gañjana ll

Lord Balaram, of the strength of a crore (ten million) lions, | And also lying there is, Kaliya (Lord Krishna).

ସାତଗୋଟି ପର୍ବତରୁ ଅଟଇ ଯେ ଗରୁ । ନାମ ବହିଅଛନ୍ତି ଅଚଳ ମହାମେରୁ ॥

Sātagoṭi parvataru aṭa'i je garu | Nāma bahi'achanti acala mahāmeru ll

Heavier than seven mountains is the weight of the body (referring to the Lords). | They are bearing the name of the immovable great Meru mountain.

ମହାଲକ୍ଷ୍ମୀ ବୋଇଲେରେ ଏମନ୍ତ କରିବ । ଦଉଡ଼ିଆ ଖଟ ଏକ ଗୋଟି ଯେ ଆଣିବ ॥

Mahālakṣmī boilere emanta kariba | Da'udiā khaṭa eka goṭi je āṇiba ॥

Mahalakshmi said — do like this now: | Bring a moving cot (a wheeled or mobile cot).

ରାମକୃଷ୍ଣ ଦୁହିଁଙ୍କୁ ଯେ ଗଡ଼ାଇଣ ଦେବ । ଶୋଇବାର ରତ୍ନଖଟ ବୋହିଣ ଆଣିବ ॥

Rāmakṛuṣṇa duhiṅku je gaḍā'iṇa deba | Shoibāra ratnakhata bohina āṇiba ॥

Transfer both Ram and Krishna (the brothers) from one cot to another. | Then carry and bring back the gem-studded cot meant for sleeping.

ଏହାଶୁଣି ବେତାଳ ଯେ ଶୀଘ୍ର ଚଳିଗଲେ । ରତ୍ନଖଟ ପାଶେ ଦଉଡ଼ିଆ ଖଟ ଦେଲେ ॥

Ehāśuṇi betāḷa je śīghra caligale | Ratnakhata pāśe da'udiā khaṭa dele ॥

Hearing this, the Vetalas immediately went off (hurriedly left). | They placed the moving cot beside the gem-studded cot.

ବଳରାମଙ୍କୁ ପ୍ରଥମେ ଧଇଲେକ ଯାଇ । ଦଉଡ଼ିଆ ଖଟକୁ ଯେ ଦେଲେ ଗଡ଼ିଆଇ ॥

Baḷarāmaṅku prathame dhaileka jā'i | Da'udiā khaṭaku je dele gaḍi'ā'i ॥

First, they lifted Balaram and went (toward the new cot). | And transferred him onto the wheeled cot.

ଏ ଉତ୍ତାରୁ ଜଗନ୍ନାଥ ପ୍ରଭୁଙ୍କୁ ଧଇଲେ । ଦଉଡ଼ିଆ ଖଟ ଉପରକୁ ଗଡ଼ାଇଲେ ॥

E uttāru Jagannātha prabhuṅku dhaile | Da'uṛiā khaṭa uparaku gaḍāile ॥

Then they lifted Lord Jagannath from the other side. | And laid him onto the wheeled cot.

ଶୋଇବାର ରତ୍ନଖଟ ଆଣିଲେକ ବୋହି । ମହାଲକ୍ଷ୍ମୀ ଆଗେ ହେଲେ ଆନନ୍ଦରେ ନେଇ ॥

Shoibāra ratnakhata āṇileka bohi | Mahālakṣmī āge hele ānandare nei ॥

They brought back the sleeping gem-studded cot by carrying it away. | They placed it in front of Mahalakshmi, joyfully.

ବଳରାମ ପିନ୍ଧିବାର ପାଟ ବୋହି ନେଲେ । ଜଗନ୍ନାଥ ପିନ୍ଧିବାର ନେତ ଘେନିଗଲେ ॥

Baḷarāma pindhibāra pāṭa bohi nele | Jagannātha pindhibāra neta ghenigale ॥

They brought the attire meant for dressing Balaram. | And took the cloth (headwrap or attire) meant for dressing Jagannath.

ଦେଖିକରି ମହାଲକ୍ଷ୍ମୀ ସନ୍ତୁଷ୍ଟ ହୋଇଲେ । ଅଷ୍ଟବେତାଳଙ୍କୁ ବର ଯାଚିଣ ଯେ ଦେଲେ ॥

Dekhikari Mahālakṣmī santuṣṭa hoile | Aṣṭabetāḷaṅku bara jāciṇa je dele ॥

Seeing (this), Mahalakshmi became satisfied. | She gave a boon by asking the eight Vetalas to choose (a wish).

ଆରେ ଅଷ୍ଟବେତାଳରେ ଏମନ୍ତ କରିବ । ବୈକୁଣ୍ଠପୁରରେ ଯାଇଁ ସୁଖରେ ରହିବ ॥

Āre aṣṭabetāḷare emanta kariba | Vaikunthapurare jā'in sukhare rahiba ॥

Oh eight Vetalas, do this (task). | Go to Vaikunthapur and live there happily.

ଆଜ୍ଞା ପାଇଣ ବେତାଳଗଣ ବେଗେ ଗଲେ । ବୈକୁଣ୍ଠ ପୁରରେ ଯାଇ ପ୍ରବେଶ ହୋଇଲେ ॥

Ājñā pāiṇa betāḷagaṇa bege gale | Vaikuntha purare jā'i prabeśa hoile ||

Upon receiving the command, the Vetalas quickly left. | They went to Vaikunthapur and entered (it).

ମହାଲକ୍ଷ୍ମୀ ତହୁଁ ଏକ କଥା ବିଚାରିଲେ । ସରସ୍ୱତୀ ଦେବୀଙ୍କୁ ଯ ହୃଦେ ସୁମରିଲେ ॥

Mahālakṣmī tahun eka kathā bicārile | Sarasvatī debīṅku ja hṛude sumarile ||

Thereafter, Mahalakshmi thought of one idea. | She remembered Goddess Saraswati in her heart.

ବୋଇଲେ ଗୋ ସରସ୍ୱତୀ ଏମନ୍ତ କରିବ | ରାଜ୍ୟ ରାଜ୍ୟ ହୋଇ ଘରେ ଘରେ ବୁଲୁଥିବ ॥

Boile go sarasvatī emanta kariba | Rājya rājya hoi ghare ghare buluthiba ||

She said: "O Saraswati, please do this." | "Move about from kingdom to kingdom, house to house."

ସର୍ବଦ୍ୱାରେ ଜଗନ୍ନାଥ ବୁଲିବେଟି ଯାଇଁ | ସର୍ବ କଣ୍ଠେ ସରସ୍ୱତୀ ବିଜେ କର ତୁହି ॥

Sarvadvāre Jagannātha bulibeṭi jā'in | Sarva kaṇṭhe sarasvatī bije kara tuhi ॥

Jagannath will wander, going from door to door. | You (Saraswati) take control of every throat (i.e., speech of all).

ଅନ୍ନ ପାଣି କେହି ତାଙ୍କୁ କିଛି ହିଁ ନ ଦେବେ | ଏତେ ଦୁଃଖ ପାଇଲେ ସେ ମୋତେ ସୁମରିବେ ॥

Anna pāṇi kehi tāṅku kichi hin na debe | Ete duḥkha pāile se mote sumaribe ॥

No one will give him even a bit of food or water. | When he suffers so much, then he will remember me.

ଆରାମ ଦାୟିନୀ ରାତ୍ର ସୁଖରେ ପାଇଲା | ଦିନ ଦୁଇ ଘଡ଼ିକରେ ନିଦ୍ରା ଯେ ଭାଜିଲା ॥

Ārāma dāyinī rātra sukhare pāilā | Dina dui ghadikare nidrā je bhājilā ॥

The restful night passed in comfort. | Sleep vanished at two during the day.

ବଳରାମ କହୁଛନ୍ତି ଶୁଣରେ କହ୍ନାଇ । ଗହଳ ଚହଳ ଆଜି କିଛି ଶୁଭୁନାହିଁ ॥

Baḷarāma kahuchanti śuṇare kahnā'i | Gahaḷa cahala āji kichi śubhunāhin ||

Balaram says, "Listen, O Kanhai (Krishna)." | Today there is no sound, no bustle, nothing auspicious.

ମୁଦିରଥ ପଣ୍ଡାର ତ ତୁଣ୍ଡ ଶୁଭୁ ନାହିଁ । ଦାସୀ ପରିବାରୀ ଯେ ପରିଚା ଗଲେ କାହିଁ ॥

Mudiratha paṇḍāra ta tuṇḍa śubhu nāhin | Dāsī paribārī je paricā gale kāhin ||

The mouths of the Mudiratha Pandas (temple servitors) are not making any sound. | Why have the maidservants and attendants all gone away?

ଶ୍ରୀମୁଖ ପଖାଳିବାକୁ ଜଳ ନ ମିଳଇ । କି ବୁଦ୍ଧି କରିବା ଏବେ କହରେ କହ୍ନାଇଁ ॥

Śrīmukha pakhāḷibāku jaḷa na miḷai | Ki buddhi karibā ebe kahare kahnā'in ||

There is no water even to wash the divine mouth. | What should we do now? Tell me, O Kanhai (Krishna).

ଜଗନ୍ନାଥ କହୁଛନ୍ତି ଶୁଣ ଜ୍ୟେଷ୍ଠଭାଇ । ଲକ୍ଷ୍ମୀ ଛାଡ଼ିଗଲାରୁ ଯେ ଏମନ୍ତ ହୁଅଇ ॥

Jagannātha kahuchanti śuṇa jyeṣṭhabhā'i | Lakṣmī chāṛigālāru je emanta hu'ai ll

Jagannath says, "Listen, elder brother." | Since Lakshmi has left, all this is happening.

ବଳରାମ କହୁଛନ୍ତି ଶୁଣିରେ କହ୍ନାଇ । ଭାର୍ଯ୍ୟା ଛାର ଏମନ୍ତକୁ କହୁଅଛୁ ତୁହି ॥

Baḷarāma kahuchanti śuṇire kahnā'i | Bhārjyā chāra emantaku kahu'achu tuhi ll

Balaram says, "Listen, O Kanhai (Krishna)." | You left your wife, and this is what you are now facing.

କାହାର ଭାରିଯା ଯେବେ ଋଷି ହଜିଯାଏ । ତାର ଗୃହସ୍ଥ କି ଭାତ ରାନ୍ଧିଣ ନଖାଏ ॥

Kāhāra bhārijā jebe ṛṣi haji jāe | Tāra gṛuhastha ki bhāta rāndhiṇa nakhāe ll

When someone's wife becomes angry or goes away, | Then doesn't that householder eat cooked rice?

ଭଣ୍ଡାର ଘରକୁ ବିଜେକଲେ ଦୁଇଭାଇ । ଭଣ୍ଡାରେ ଦେଖିଲେ କିଛି ପଦାର୍ଥ ଯେ ନାହିଁ ॥

Bhaṇḍāra gharaku bijekale duibhā'i | Bhaṇḍāre dekhile kichi padārtha je nāhin ||

The two brothers went together to the store room. | In the storehouse, they saw that there were no provisions at all.

ବଳରାମ କହୁଛନ୍ତି କାହିଁ କିସହେଲା । ବାଉନ କୋଟି ଭଣ୍ଡାର କେ ଘେନିଣ ଗଲା ॥

Baḷarāma kahuchanti kāhin kisahēlā | Bā'una koṭi bhaṇḍāra ke ghenina galā ||

Balaram said, "Why and how did this happen?" | Who took away the fifty-two crore-worth storehouse?

ଲକ୍ଷେ ଜୀବ ଖାଇଲେ ବୋହିଲେ ନ ସରଇ । କ୍ଷଣକ ଭିତରେ କିଏ ଘେନିଗଲା ବୋହି ॥

Lakṣe jība khāile bohile na sarai | Kṣaṇaka bhitare ki'e ghenigala bohī ||

Even if a lakh beings ate, they couldn't carry it all away. | Who carried it all away within a moment?

ସୁବର୍ଣ୍ଣ ମୁଦିଏ ବଳରାମ ଯେ ପାଇଲେ | ସାତଗୋଟି ଗଣ୍ଠିଦେଇ କାନିରେ ବାନ୍ଧିଲେ ॥

Subarṇa mudie Baḷarāma je pāile | Sātagoṭi ganṭhide'i kānire bāndhile ॥

Balaram found a golden coin there. | After tying seven knots, it was fastened to the end of his cloth.

ଜଗନ୍ନାଥ କହନ୍ତି ଯେ କି ପାଇଲ ଭାଇ । ବଳରାମ କହୁଛନ୍ତି ଧନ ପାଇଲଇଁ ॥

Jagannātha kahanti je ki pāila bhā'i | Baḷarāma kahuchanti dhana pāila'in ॥

Jagannath says: "What did you get, brother?" | Balaram replies: "I got some wealth."

ଜଗନ୍ନାଥ କହୁଛନ୍ତି ବଳରାମ ଭାଇ । ବେଙ୍ଗିପିତ୍ତଳ ଖଣ୍ଡକ ରଖ କାହିଁପାଇଁ ॥

Jagannātha kahuchanti baḷarāma bhā'i | Beṅgipittṭala khanḍaka rakha kāhin pā'in ॥

Jagannath says: "Brother Balaram..." | "...why are you keeping pieces of brass?"

ବଳରାମ କହୁଛନ୍ତି କି କଥା ଘଟିଲା । ପାଇଥିବା ସ୍ୱର୍ଣ୍ଣ ବେଙ୍ଗି ପିତ୍ତଳ ହୋଇଲା ॥

Baḷarāma kahuchanti ki kathā ghaṭilā | Pāithibā svarṇa beṅgi pittṭala hoilā ||

Balaram replies: "What are you saying, what happened?" | "The gold I had found has now turned into a piece of brass!"

ଶୁଦ୍ଧ ସୁବର୍ଣ୍ଣରୁ ଯେଉଁ ଧନ ହୋଇଥଲା । କାଣି କଉଡ଼ି କଡ଼ାକୁ ସମାନ ନୋହିଲା ॥

Śuddha subarṇaru jeun dhana hoithalā | Kāṇi ka'udi kaḍāku samāna nohila ||

"The wealth that was once pure gold..." | "...is now not even worth a broken cowrie or a worn-out coin!"

ସେଠାରୁ ବାହାରି ଗଲେ ଦୁଇଗୋଟି ଭାଇ | ପାକଶାଳ ଦୁଆରେ ଯେ ପ୍ରବେଶିଲେ ଯାଇ ॥

Seṭhāru bāhāri gale duigoṭi bhā'i | Pākāṣāḷa duāre je prabeśile jā'i ||

From there, the two brothers went out. | They approached and entered the kitchen doorway.

ବଳରାମ ଠିଆ ହେଲେ ଦୁଆର ମୁହଁକୁ । ଜଗନ୍ନାଥ ପଶିଗଲେ ରୋଷାଇ ଘରକୁ ॥

Baḷarāma ṭhiā hele duāra mukhanku | Jagannātha paśigale roṣāi gharaku ll

Balaram stood at the door's entrance. | Jagannath went inside the cooking room (kitchen).

ଦେହରେ ଲାଗିଲା କଳା ମୁହଁରେ ଲାଗିଲା । କଳା ଶ୍ରୀମୁଖ ଗୋଟିକ ଝଟକି ଦିଶିଲା ॥

Dehare lāgilā kaḷā muhare lāgilā | Kaḷā śrīmukha goṭika jhaṭaki diśilā ll

Black soot touched their bodies and faces. | On the black divine face, a small sparkle appeared.

ବଳରାମ କହୁଛନ୍ତି ଶୁଣ ଜଗନ୍ନାଥ । ବଡ଼ ଖିଆ ବୋଲି ତତେ କହନ୍ତି ଜଗତ ॥

Baḷarāma kahuchanti śuṇa Jagannātha | Baḍa khiā boli tate kahanti jagata ll

Balaram says, "Listen, Jagannath..." | "The world calls you a great glutton!"

ମତେ ଅନ୍ନ ନ ଦେଇଣ ସବୁ ଖାଉ ତୁହି । ଜଗନ୍ନାଥ କହୁଛନ୍ତି ଶୁଣ ଜ୍ୟେଷ୍ଠ ଭାଇ ॥

Mate anna na deiṇa sabu khā'u tuhi | Jagannātha kahuchanti śuṇa jyeṣṭha bhā'i ll

"You don't give me food, you eat everything yourself!" | Jagannath replies, "Listen, elder brother..."

ଅନ କାହିଁ ମିଳିବ ଯେ ଚୁଲି ସୁଦ୍ଧା ନାହିଁ । ନ ବୁଝି ଏପରି କିମ୍ପା କହୁଛ ଗୋସାଇଁ ॥

Ana kāhin miḷiba je culi suddhā nāhin | Na bujhi epari kimpā kahucha gosā'in ll

"Where will I get rice when there isn't even a cooking stove left?" | "Why are you saying such things without understanding, dear brother?"

ସେଠାରୁ ଯାଇ ଦେଖିଲେ ଧାନର ମରାଇ | ଲକ୍ଷ ଲକ୍ଷ ଭରଣ ଯେ ଧାନ ତହିଁ ଥାଇ ॥

Seṭhāru jā'i dekhile dhānara marā'i | Lakṣa lakṣa bharaṇa je dhāna tahin thā'i ll

From there, they went and saw the rice storage barn (grain depot). | Hundreds of thousands of measures of rice used to lie there.

ଦେଖିଲେ ଅଗାଡ଼ି ତହିଁ ଗୋଟିଏ ଯେ ନାହିଁ । ତହୁଁଗଲେ ଦୁଇଭାଇ ନିରାଶ ଯେ ହୋଇ ॥

Dekhile agāḍi tahin goṭie je nāhin | Tahun gale duibhā'i nirāśa je hoi ||

But not a single grain (handful) was visible on the surface. | The two brothers went away from there, feeling disappointed.

ଇନ୍ଦ୍ରଦ୍ୟୁମ୍ନ କୂଳେ ଯାଇ ପ୍ରବେଶ ହୋଇଲେ । ଟୋପାଏଟୋପାଏ ଯେପାଣି ତହିଁ ନ ଦେଖିଲେ ॥

Indradyumna kūḷe jā'i prabeśa hoile | Ṭopā'eṭopā'e jepāṇi tahin na dekhile ||

They entered (arrived) at the bank of the Indradyumna lake. | They didn't see even a drop of water there.

ବଡ଼ ଦେଉଳରେ ଯାଇ ପ୍ରବେଶ ହୋଇଲେ । ସେହିଦିନ ଉପବାସ କରିଣ ରହିଲେ ॥

Baḍa deuḷare jā'i prabeśa hoile | Sehidina upabāsa kariṇa rahile ||

They entered the big temple (main shrine). | They remained fasting that entire day.

ବେଳ ଦୁଇ ଘଡ଼ିକରେ ନିଦ୍ରା ଯେ ଭାଙ୍ଗିଲା ।ମୁଖ ପ୍ରକ୍ଷାଳନ ଅର୍ଥେ ପାଣି ନ ମିଳିଲା ॥

Beḷa dui ghaḍikare nidrā je bhāṅgilā | Mukha prakṣālana arthe pāṇi na miḷilā ll

After two, during the day, their sleep was broken. | They didn't find water even to wash their faces.

କି ବୁଦ୍ଧି କରିବା ଏବେ ବୁଦ୍ଧି ଦିଶୁନାହିଁ । ବଳରାମ କହୁଛନ୍ତି ଶୁଣରେ କହ୍ନାଇ ॥

Ki buddhi karibā ebe buddhi diśunāhin | Baḷarāma kahuchanti śuṇare kahnā'i ll

What decision to take now – no sense (wisdom) was appearing. | Balaram says, "Listen, dear Kanhai (Krishna)..."

କାଲି ଉପବାସରେ ରହିଲେ ବେନିଭାଇ । ଆଜି ପାଦେ ଯିବାକୁ ତ ବଳ ପାଉନାହିଁ ॥

Kāli upavāsare rahile benibhā'i | Āji pāde jibāku ta baḷa pā'unāhin ll

Yesterday, both the brothers (referring to Jagannath and Himself) remained fasting. | Today, there is no strength even to walk on foot.

କେଉଁଠାରୁ ଯେବେ ଆଜି ନ ମିଳିବ ଅନ୍ନ । କେମନ୍ତ ପ୍ରକାରେ ଆମ୍ଭେ ଧରିବା ଜୀବନ ॥

Keunṭhāru jebe āji na miḷiba anna | Kemaṁta prakāre āmbhe dharibā jībana ll

If we don't get any food anywhere today... | Then how will we sustain our lives?

ବଳରାମ କହୁଛନ୍ତି ଶୁଣ ଆରେ ବାବା । ନଗରରେ ଭିକ୍ଷା ମାଗି ଜୀବନ ପୋଷିବା ॥

Baḷarāma kahuchanti śuṇa āre bābā | Nagarare bhikṣā māgi jībana pōṣibā ll

Balaram says, "Listen, dear brother." | We will go to the city and sustain our lives by begging alms.

କାନ୍ଧରେ ପକାଇ ଛିଣ୍ଡା ଉତ୍ତରୀ ପଇତା । ହସ୍ତରେ ଧଇଲେ ଦୁଇଭାଇ ଭଙ୍ଗାଛତା ॥

Kāndhare pakāi chindā uttarī pa'itā | Hastare dhaile duibhā'i bhaṅgāchatā ll

Wearing torn upper garments and sacred thread on their shoulders... | The two brothers held broken umbrellas in their hands.

ଚିତା ଘେନିବାକୁ ଜଳ କାହିଁ ନ ପାଆନ୍ତି । ଯାହା ଘର ଠାକୁ ପାଣି ମାଗିବାକୁ ଯାନ୍ତି ॥

Citā ghenibāku jaḷa kāhin na pā'ānti | Jāhā ghara ṭhāku pāṇi māgibāku jānti ॥

They don't even get water to apply tilak on their forehead. | From whichever house they go to ask for water..

ଚୋର ଖଣ୍ଟ ବୋଲି ମାରି ଘଉଡ଼ାଇ ଦ୍ୟନ୍ତି | ସେଠାବରୁ ଦୁଇଭାଇ ଭୟେ ପଳାବନ୍ତି ॥

Cora khaṇta boli māri gha'uḍā'i dyanti | Seṭhābaru duibhā'i bhaye paḷābanti ॥

They beat and drive them away saying "thieves and burglars!" | From there, the two brothers flee out of fear.

ଜଗନ୍ନାଥ କହୁଛନ୍ତି ଶୁଣ ଜ୍ୟେଷ୍ଠ ଭାଇ । ବଡ଼ ପଣ୍ଡା ଘରକୁ ହେ ଚାଲ ଏବେ ଯାଇ ॥

Jagannātha kahuchanti śuṇa jyeṣṭha bhā'i | Baḍa paṇḍā gharaku he cāla ebe jā'i ॥

Jagannath says, "Listen, elder brother..." | Let us go now to the house of the chief priest (Bada Panda)

ହସ୍ତ ଧରାଧରି ହୋଇ ଦୁଇ ଭାଇ ଗଲେ । ବଡ଼ପଣ୍ଡା ଘରଠାରେ ପ୍ରବେଶ ହୋଇଲେ ॥

Hasta dharādhari hoi dui bhāi gale | Baḍapaṇḍā gharathāre prabeśa hoile ll

Hand in hand, the two brothers went. | They entered the house of the chief priest (Bada Panda).

ବଧୂ ତାର କହଇ ଯେ ଶାଶୁ ଆଗେ ଯାଇ । ବ୍ରାହ୍ମଣ ଯେ ଦୁଇଗୋଟି ଆସିଛନ୍ତି ଧାଇଁ ॥

Badhū tāra kahai je śāśu āge jāi | Brāhmaṇa je duigoṭi āsichanti dhā'in ll

His daughter-in-law says, "Go to mother-in-law first." | "Two Brahmins have come running," she says.

ଶାଶୁ ରାଣ୍ଡି ତାହାଙ୍କୁ ଯେ ଚିହ୍ନି ନ ପାରିଲା । ଧାଇଁ ଯାଇ ବେଗେ ଦାଣ୍ଡ କବାଟ କିଳିଲା ॥

Śāśu rāṇḍi tāhāṅku je cihni na pārilā | Dhā'in jāi bege dāṇḍa kabāṭa kiḷilā ll

The widow mother-in-law couldn't recognize them. | She ran quickly and slammed the door shut.

ଆସ ଆସ ବୋହୂଏ ଲୋ ଠେଙ୍ଗା ବାଡ଼ିଧରି । ଚୋର କି ଖଣ୍ଟ ଏ ଦୁହେଁ ଦେବା ଆଡ଼କରି ॥

Āsa āsa bohū'e lo theṅgā bāṛidhari | Cora ki khaṇṭa e duhen debā ādakari ll

"Come, come, daughters-in-law, bring the stick," she said. | "Are these thieves or robbers? Let's beat them both!"

ଏହାଶୁଣି ଦୁଇ ଭାଇ ତହୁଁ ପଳାଇଲେ । ସାମବେଦ ଯଜୁର୍ବେଦ ଦୂରେ ଉଚ୍ଚାରିଲେ ॥

Ehāśuṇi dui bhāi tahun paḷāile | Sāmabeda jajurveda dūre ucchārile ll

Hearing this, the two brothers fled from there. | From afar, they chanted verses from the Sama Veda and Yajur Veda.

ଶୁଣି ଶୁଷ୍କ ତରୁଗଣ ପଲ୍ଲବୀ ଉଠିଲେ । ଭିକ୍ଷୁକ ବ୍ରାହ୍ମଣ ବୋଲି ବ୍ରାହ୍ମଣୀ ଚିହ୍ନିଲେ ॥

Śuṇi śuṣka tarugaṇa pallavī uṭhile | Bhikṣuka brāhmaṇa boli brāhmaṇī cihnile ll

Hearing (this), the dry trees sprouted leaves (a metaphor expressing sudden joy or positive transformation). | Recognizing them as begging Brahmins, the Brahmin woman identified them.

ଦୁଇ ଭାଇଙ୍କୁ ସେ ଡାକି ତହିଁ ବସାଇଲା । ଖୁଦ ମଲୁଖ ମିଶାଇ ସତ୍ୱର ରାନ୍ଧିଲା ॥

Dui bhāiṅku se ḍāki tahin basāilā | Khuda maḷukha miśāi satvara rāndhilā ||

She called the two brothers and made them sit there. | She quickly cooked rice by mixing broken rice and coarse grains.

ଅଫିଟା କଦଳୀମଞ୍ଜ ଦୁଇଖଣ୍ଡ ଆଣି । ବେନି ଭାଇ ପକାଇଣ ସିଞ୍ଚିଲେକ ପାଣି ॥

Aphiṭā kadaḷīmañja duikhaṇḍa āṇi | Beni bhāi pakāiṇa siñcileka pāṇi ||

She brought two pieces of overripe banana plantain flower stalk. | Beni Bhai (referring to the Lords), she cooked and sprinkled water (prepared them for offering).

କଂସା ଘେନି ବ୍ରାହ୍ମଣୀ ଯେ ଅନ୍ନ ଆଣିଗଲା । ଅନ୍ନ କି ବାଢ଼ିବ ତାର ହାଣ୍ଡି ଉଭାହେଲା ॥

Kansā gheni brāhmaṇī je anna āṇigala | Anna ki bāṛhibā tāra hāṇḍi ubhāhela ||

The Brahmin woman brought the food in a bronze vessel. | Forget about serving the rice, the pot itself vanished.

ଲକ୍ଷ୍ମୀଦ୍ରୋହୀ ପୁରୁଷ ଏ ବୋଲିଣ ଜାଣିଲା | ପାକଶାଳରୁ ଲେଉଟି ପାଶରେ ମିଳିଲା ॥

Lakṣmīdrohī puruṣa e boliṇa jāṇilā | Pākāṣāḷaru le'uṭi pāśare miḷilā ॥

She came to know: "These are men who are abandoned by Lakshmi." | She returned from the kitchen and sat down beside them.

ଦୁଇଗୋଟି ଭାଇଙ୍କର ହସ୍ତକୁ ଧଇଲା । କଟୁକଥା କହି ତାଙ୍କୁ ଦାଣ୍ଡରେ ଛାଡ଼ିଲା ॥

Duigoṭi bhāiṅkara hastaku dhaile | Kaṭukathā kahi tāṅku dāṇḍare chāḍilā ॥

She held the hands of the two brothers. | Speaking harsh words, she left them at the doorstep.

ତହୁଁ ଦୁଇଜଣ ଯେ ନିରାଶ ହୋଇଗଲେ । କବୀର ସାହିରେ ଯାଇ ପ୍ରବେଶ ହୋଇଲେ ॥

Tahun duijaṇa je nirāśa hoigale | Kabīra sāhire jāi prabeśa hoile ॥

Thereupon, the two became disheartened and left. | They went and entered the street of Kabir (the poet or sage).

କ୍ଷୁଧାର୍ତ୍ତ ବ୍ରାହ୍ମଣ ବୋଲି କବୀର ଜାଣିଲେ । ଖଇ ଚାରି ପାଞ୍ଚ ମାଣ ଆଣି ବେଗେ ଦେଲେ ॥

Kṣudhārtta brāhmaṇa boli kabīra jāṇile | Khai cāri pāñca māṇa āṇi bege dele ॥

Kabir recognized them as hungry Brahmins. | He quickly brought and gave four or five measures of puffed paddy.

ଅନୁର୍ଗତେ ଜାଣିଲେ ଯେ ଦେବୀ କମଳିନୀ । ପବନକୁ ଡାକି ଆଜ୍ଞାଦେଲେ ସେହିକ୍ଷଣି ॥

Anurgate jāṇile je Devī kamaḷinī | Pavanaku ḍāki ājñādele sehi kṣaṇi ॥

Goddess Kamalini (Lakshmi) came to know through her inner intuition. | She instantly called the wind (Pavan) and gave him a command.

ଆରେ ପବନ ତୁହି ତ ବେଗେ ଚଳିଯିବୁ । ଖଇ ଚାରି ପାଞ୍ଚ ମାଣ ଉଡ଼ାଇଣ ନେବୁ ॥

Āre paban tuhi ta bege calijibu | Khai cāri pāñca māṇa udāiṇa nebu ॥

"O Pavan, you must go immediately." | "Fly away and take those four or five measures of puffed paddy."

ଆଜ୍ଞା ପାଇ ପବନ ଯେ ବେଗେ ଚଳିଗଲା । ପ୍ରଭୁଙ୍କ ଆଗରୁ ଖଇ ଉଡ଼ାଇଣ ନେଲା ॥

Ājñā pāi pavan je bege caligala | Prabhuṅka āguru khala udāiṇa nelā ॥

Receiving the command, Pavan (the wind) quickly went. | He flew off and took away the puffed paddy from in front of the Lord.

ବଳରାମ କହୁଛନ୍ତି ଶୁଣରେ କହ୍ନାଇ । ପ୍ରାଣଗଲା ବେଳେ ଜାତିକୁଳ ଲୋଡୁକାହିଁ ॥

Baḷarāma kahuchanti śuṇare kahnā'i | Prāṇagalā beḷe jāti kuḷa loḍukāhin ॥

Balaram says, "Listen, my dear Kanhai (Krishna)." | "When life is at stake, why worry about caste or lineage?"

ପଦ୍ମ ପୋଖରୀକୁ ଚାଲ ଯିବା ବେନି ଭାଇ । ପଦ୍ମମୂଳ ଖାଇ ପ୍ରାଣ ବଞ୍ଚାଇବା ତହିଁ ॥

Padma pokharīku cāla jibā beni bhā'i | Padmamūḷa khāi prāṇa bañcāibā tahin ॥

"Let us go to the lotus pond, dear brother." | "We'll eat lotus roots there and preserve our lives."

ଫଳ ପୁଷ୍ପ କରି ତହୁଁ ଗୁଡ଼ାଏ ଆଣିବା । ଅଧିକ ମିଳିଲେ କିଛି ସଞ୍ଚିଣ ରଖିବା ॥

Phaḷa puṣpa kari tahun guḍāe āṇibā | Adhika miḷile kichi sañciṇa rakhībā ll

"We will gather some fruits and flowers from there." | "If we get more, we will store some for later."

ଏମନ୍ତ ବିଚାର କରି ଦୁଇଭାଇ ଗଲେ । ପଦ୍ମ ପୁଷ୍କରିଣୀରେ ଯେ ପ୍ରବେଶ ହୋଇଲେ ॥

Emanta bicāra kari duibhāi gale | Padma puṣkariṇīre je prabeśa hoile ll

Thinking thus, the two brothers went. | They entered into the lotus pond.

ପଦ୍ମପୋଖରୀରେ ସାତ ତାଳ ପାଣି ଥିଲା । ଲକ୍ଷ୍ମୀ ଆଜ୍ଞା ମାତ୍ରେ ସବୁ ପଙ୍କ ହୋଇଗଲା ॥

Padmapokharīre sāta tāḷa pāṇi thilā | Lakṣmī ājñā mātre sabu paṅka hoigala ll

In the lotus pond, there was water seven palm-depths deep. | By Lakshmi's command alone, all of it turned to mud

ଜଗନ୍ନାଥ କହୁଛନି କି ବୁଦ୍ଧି କରିବା । ଜଳ ନାହିଁ ଫଳ ଏଥି କାହୁଁବା ପାଇବା ॥

Jagannātha kahuchani ki buddhi karibā | Jaḷa nāhin phaḷa ethi kāhunbā pāibā ll

Jagannath says, "What decision should we make now?" | "There is no water, and how will we even get fruit here?"

ଏହା କହି ଦୁଇଜଣ ତହୁଁ ଚଳିଗଲେ । ଯାଉ ଯାଉ ବାଟେ ଏକ ଯୋଗୀକି ଭେଟିଲେ ॥

Ehā kahi duijaṇa tahun caligale | Jāu jāu bāṭe eka jogīki bheṭile ll

Saying this, the two of them departed from there. | While walking on the path, they happened to meet a yogi.

ଜଗନ୍ନାଥ କହୁଛନ୍ତି ଶୁଣ ଆହେ ନାଥ । ତୁମ୍ଭର ଥାଳରୁ ଯେ ଆମ୍ଭଙ୍କୁ ଦିଅ ଭାତ ॥

Jagannātha kahuchanti śuṇa āhe nātha | Tumbhara thāḷaru je āmbhanku dia bhāta ll

Jagannath says, "Listen, O respected Nath (Master)." | "Please give us rice from your plate."

ସତ୍ୟାନନ୍ଦ ବୋଲେ ରାମକୃଷ୍ଣ ମୁଖ ଚାହିଁ । ଲକ୍ଷ୍ମୀ ଦ୍ରୋହୀ ହୋଇଅଛ ତୁମ୍ଭେ ଦୁଇ ଭାଇ ॥

Satyānanda bole Rāmakṛuṣṇa mukha cāhin | Lakṣmī drohī hoiachha tumbhe dui bhā'i ॥

Satyānanda (the yogi) spoke, looking at Ramakrishna's face. | "You two brothers have become traitors to Lakshmi."

ଦୁଧ ଅନ୍ନରେ ଯେ ମୋର ଥାଳ ପୁରିଥିଲା । ତୁମ୍ଭେ ମାଗନ୍ତେଣ ଅନ୍ତ ଶୂନ୍ୟ ହୋଇଗଲା ॥

Dudha annare je mora thāḷa purithilā | Tumbhe māganteṇa anta śūnya hoigala ॥

My plate was filled with milk and rice. | But when you begged, it became completely empty.

ଅନ୍ନ ଜଳ ନ ମିଳିବ ତୁମ୍ଭଙ୍କୁ ଯେ କାହିଁ । ସମୁଦ୍ର କୂଳକୁ ବେଗେ ଯାଅ ଦୁଇଭାଇ ॥

Anna jaḷa na miḷiba tumbhanku je kāhin | Samudra kūḷaku bege jā'o duibhā'i ॥

You will not receive food or water from anyone. | Quickly go to the seashore, both of you brothers.

ମୁହିଁ ଯାଇଥିଲି ମୋତେ ଅନ୍ନ ଥିଲେ ଦେଇ । ଖାଇଲେ ବହିଲେ ସେହି ଅନ୍ନ ନ ସରଇ ॥

Muhin jāithili mote anna thile dei | Khāile bahile sehi anna na sarai ॥

When I went there, I received food... | ...if you eat from it and carry it, that food shall never be depleted.

ଏହି ରୁପେ ସତ୍ୟାନନ୍ଦ ବାଟ କହିଦେଲେ | ଯିବା ବୋଲି ଦୁଇଭାଇ କମର ବାନ୍ଧିଲେ ॥

Ehi rupe satyānanda bāṭa kahidele | Jibā boli duibhāi kamara bāndhile ॥

In this way, Satyānanda described the path (route). | Saying "let's go," the two brothers tied their waists (got ready for the journey).

ହଟି କମଳିନୀ ତହୁଁ ହଟ ଭିଆଇଲେ | ସୂର୍ଯ୍ୟଙ୍କୁ ରାଇଣ ଦେବୀ ବେଗେ ଆଜ୍ଞା ଦେଲେ ॥

Haṭi kamaḷinī tahun haṭa bhiāile | Sūryaṅku rāiṇa Devī bege ājñā dele ॥

Seeing that, Goddess Kamalini became agitated (or upset). | The queenly Goddess immediately gave orders to the Sun.

ଅତିଶୀଘ୍ର ଟାଣଖରା କର ତୁମ୍ଭେ ଯାଇ | ବାଲି ମାଟି ତାତୁ ବେଗେ ଡହ ଡହ ହୋଇ ॥

Atiśīghra ṭāṇakhārā kara tumbhe jāi | Bāli māṭi tātu bege ḍaha ḍaha hoi ॥

Go quickly and make intense heat. | Make the sand and soil boil and burn quickly (make it scorching hot).

ତାତିବ ଖରାରେ ଯେହ୍ନେ ଭାଜିବାର ବାଲି | ପାଦେ ମାତ୍ର କେହି ତହିଁ ନ ପାରିବେ ଚାଲି ॥

Tātiba kharāre jehne bhājibāra bāli | Pāde mātra kehi tahin na pāribe cāli ॥

In that heat, the sand will fry like in a pan. | No one will be able to walk even with bare feet there.

ଜଗନ୍ନାଥ କହୁଛନ୍ତି ଶୁଣ ଜ୍ୟେଷ୍ଠ ଭାଇ । ଏତେ ବଡ଼ ଖରାରେ ମୁଁ ଚାଲି ନ ପାରଇ ॥

Jagannātha kahuchanti śuṇa jyeṣṭha bhāi | Ete baḍa kharāre mun cāli na pārai ॥

Jagannāth says: Listen, elder brother. | In such intense heat, I cannot walk.

ବେଗ ବେଗ ହୋଇ ତୁମ୍ଭେ ଯାଉଅଛ ଧାଇଁ । ବୁଦ୍ଧି ଦିଶୁନାହିଁ ଏବେ କିସ କରିବଇଁ ॥

Bega bega hoi tumbhe jāu'achha dhā'in | Buddhi diśunāhin ebe kisa karibain ॥

You are rushing hurriedly, running fast. | I don't understand now what to do.

ଶୁଣି ନ ଶୁଣିଲା ପରି ବଳଦେବ ଗଲେ । କମଳାଙ୍କ ସିଂହଦ୍ୱାରେ ପ୍ରବେଶ ହୋଇଲେ ॥

Śuṇi na śuṇilā pari Baḷadeva gale | Kamaḷāṅka siṁhadvāre prabeśa hoile ॥

As if not hearing (ignoring), Baladeva went ahead. | He entered the lion gate (main entrance) of Kamalā's (Goddess Lakshmi) palace.

ସିଂହଦ୍ୱାରେ ପ୍ରବେଶିଣ ଡ଼ାକିଲେକ ଯହୁଁ । ଡାକ ଶୁଣି ଦାସୀମାନେ ଅଇଲେକ ତହୁଁ ॥

Siṁhadvāre prabeṣiṇa ḍākileka jahun | Ḍāka śuṇi dāsīmāne aileka tahun ॥

Entering the lion gate, he called out right there. | Hearing the call, the maidservants came there.

କେଉଁ ଦାସୀ କହୁଅଛି ଶୁଣ ଆଗୋ ସହି । ଏପରି କାଙ୍ଗାଳ ମୁଁ ଯେ କାହିଁ ଦେଖି ନାହିଁ ॥

Keun dāsī kahu'achhi śuṇa āgo sahi | Epari kāṅgāḷa mun je kāhin dekhi nāhin ॥

One maidservant said, "Listen, dear lady..." | I've never seen such a beggar before!

ଏହିପରି ମୋଟା ହୋଇ ଗୋଟାଏକ ଥିଲା । ଆମ୍ଭ ଠାକୁରାଣୀଙ୍କୁ ଯେ ଘରୁ ତଡ଼ି ଦେଲା ॥

Ehipari moṭā hoi goṭāeka thilā | Āmbha ṭhākurāṇīṅku je gharu tadi delā ॥

Someone so fat like this was once there... | ...who chased away our Goddess (Lakshmi) from the house!

ଏହି ରୂପେ ଦାସୀମାନେ କୁହାକୁହି ହେଲେ । ବେକରେ ହାତ ଦେଇଣ ଦାଣ୍ଡରେ ଛାଡ଼ିଲେ ॥

Ehi rupe dāsīmāne kuhākuhi hele | Bekare hāta deiṇa dāṇḍare chāḍilo ॥

In this way, the maidservants kept speaking repeatedly among each other. | They pushed him by the back (neck) and released (drove) him into the street.

ବଳରାମ ପ୍ରଭୁ ତହିଁ ଲେଉଟି ଅଇଲେ । ଜଗନ୍ନାଥ ଠାକୁରଙ୍କୁ ବାଟରେ ଦେଖିଲେ ॥

Baḷarāma prabhu tahin le'uṭi aile | Jagannātha ṭhākuraṅku bāṭare dekhile ll

Lord Balaram returned from there and came back. | He saw Lord Jagannath on the road.

ବଳରାମ କହୁଛନ୍ତି ଶୁଣରେ କହ୍ନାଇ । ଦାସୀମାନେ ଆସି ମୋତେ ଦେଲେ ଘଉଡ଼ାଇ ॥

Baḷarāma kahuchanti śuṇare kahnā'i | Dāsīmāne āsi mote dele gha'uḍā'i ll

Balaram said, "Listen, brother... Kanhai (Krishna)" | The maidservants came, beat (pushed/hit) me and drove me out.

ଜଗନ୍ନାଥ କହୁଛନ୍ତି କି ବୁଦ୍ଧି କରିବା । କେମନ୍ତ ପ୍ରକାରେ ଆମ୍ଭେ ଜୀବନ ଧରିବା ॥

Jagannātha kahuchanti ki buddhi karibā | Kemaṁta prakāre āmbhe jībana dharibā ll

Jagannath said, "What should we do now?" | How will we sustain our life like this?

ଆଉଥରେ ଚାଲ ବେନିଭାଇ ଫେରିଯିବା । ବିନୟ କରିଣ ଅନ୍ନ ଦାସୀଙ୍କୁ ମାଗିବା ॥

Āu thare cāla benibhāi pherijibā | Binaya kariṇa anna dāsīṅku māgibā ll

Let's go back again, both the brothers (Beni bhai). | We will humbly request and ask the maid for food.

ବଳରାମ କହୁଛନି ପଛେ ଆମ୍ଭେ ଥିବୁ । ଆଗରେ ଥାଇଣ ଅନ ତୁହି ଯେ ମାଗିବୁ ॥

Baḷarāma kahuchani pache āmbhe thibu | Āgare thāiṇa ana tuhi je māgibu ll

Balaram says, "I will stay behind." | You go ahead and ask for food.

ଏତେ କହି ସିଂହଦ୍ୱାରେ ପ୍ରଭୁ ବିଜେକଲେ | ମନ୍ଦିରର ଶୋଭା ଦେଖି ଆଶ୍ଚର୍ଯ୍ୟ ହୋଇଲେ ॥

Ete kahi sinhadrāre prabhu bijekale | Mandirara śobhā dekhi āścarya hoilo ll

Saying this, the Lord entered through the Lion Gate (main gate of the temple). | Seeing the grandeur of the temple, he was filled with wonder.

ବଳରାମ କହିଲେ ହେ ଶୁଣରେ କହ୍ନାଇ । ପଞ୍ଚମ ସ୍ୱରରେ ଆଗ ବେଦ ପଢ଼ ତୁହି ॥

Baḷarāma kahile he śuṇare kahnā'i | Pañca svarare āga veda paṛha tuhi II

Balaram said, "Listen, dear brother... Kanhai (Krishna)" | You chant the Vedas in the fifth note (melodiously) ahead, first.

ଜଗନ୍ନାଥ ପ୍ରଭୁ ଯହୁଁ ଏମନ୍ତ ଶୁଣିଲେ । ଓଁକାର ଶବଦ କରି ବେଦଧ୍ୱନି କଲେ ॥

Jagannātha prabhu jahun emanta śuṇile | Oṁkāra śabda kari vedadhvani kale II

When Lord Jagannath heard this... | He uttered the sacred sound "Om" and recited the Vedic chants.

ଋକ ସାମ ଯଜୁ ଅଥର୍ବ ଯେ ଚାରିବେଦ । ବ୍ରହ୍ମାଣ୍ଡ ପୁରିଉଠିଲା ଗହଗହନାଦ ॥

Rika sāma jajur atharva je cāriveda | Brahmāṇḍa puriuṭhilā gahagahanāda II

Rig, Sama, Yajur, and Atharva — the four Vedas... | The whole universe resounded with the thunderous sound.

ପଲଙ୍କ ଉପରେ ଯେ କମଳା ଶୋଇଥିଲେ । ନିସ୍ତରିଲି ନିସ୍ତରିଲି ବୋଲିଣ ବୋଇଲେ ॥

Palaṅka upare je kamaḷā shoithile | Nistarili nistarili boliṇa boile ॥

Kamala (Lakshmi) was lying on the bed. | She cried out repeatedly, "I am liberated, I am liberated."

କୋଟି କୋଟି ଜନ୍ମର ପାତକ ହେଲା କ୍ଷୟ | ମୋର ଘରେ ବିଜେ କଲେ ପ୍ରଭୁ ଦେବରାୟ ॥

Koṭi koṭi janmara pātaka helā kṣaya | Mora ghare bīja kale prabhu devarāya ॥

The sins of millions of births have been destroyed. | Because Lord Devray (Jagannath) has entered my house.

ପଚାର ପଚାର ଦାସୀ ପଚାର ଲୋ ଯାଇ । କିସ ମାଗୁଛନ୍ତି ସେ ବ୍ରାହ୍ମଣ ବେନିଭାଇ ॥

Pacāra pacāra dāsī pacāra lo jāi | Kisa māguchhanti se brāhmaṇa benibhāi ॥

"Go, go and ask," she told the maidservants repeatedly. | What are those Brahmin brothers asking for?

ଚାଲିଯାଇ ମୁଦୁସୁଲି ତାଙ୍କୁ ପଚାରିଲେ । କି ମାଗୁଛ ପଣ୍ଡାମାନେ କହ ତୁମ୍ଭେ ଭଲେ ॥

Cāli jāi mudusuli tāṅku pacārile | Ki māgucha paṇḍāmāne kaha tumbhe bhale ॥

The gentle maid went and asked them. | "O Pandas (respected Brahmins), please tell clearly what you are asking for."

ଜଗନ୍ନାଥ କହୁଛନ୍ତି ଦାସୀ ମୁଖ ଚାହିଁ । ଅନ୍ନ ଗଣ୍ଡାଏକ ତୁମ୍ଭେ ପାରିବ କି ଦେଇ ॥

Jagannātha kahuchanti dāsī mukha cāhin | Anna gaṇḍāeja tumbhe pāriba ki dei ॥

Jagannath said, looking at the maid's face... | "Can you give us even a fistful of rice?"

ଏମନ୍ତ ଶୁଣିଣ ଦାସୀମାନେ ଚଳିଗଲେ | ଲକ୍ଷ୍ମୀଠାକୁରାଣୀଆଗେବେଗେ ସେ ବୋଇଲେ ॥

Emanta śuṇiṇa dāsīmāne caligale | Lakṣmīṭhākurāṇīāgebege se boile ॥

Hearing this, the maidservants went away. | They quickly went and told it before Goddess Lakshmi.

ଦାସୀଙ୍କ ମୁଖରୁ ଯେ ଏମନ୍ତ ବାକ୍ୟ ଶୁଣି । ମନେ ବିଚାର କରନ୍ତି ଲକ୍ଷ୍ମୀ ଠାକୁରାଣୀ ॥

Dāsīṅka mukharu je emanta bākya śuṇi | Mane bicāra karanti Lakṣmī ṭhākurāṇī ll

Hearing such words from the mouths of the maidservants... | Goddess Lakshmi began contemplating in her mind.

ଏକଥା ଅରଜି ଅଛି ଚଣ୍ଡାଲୁଣି ମୁହିଁ | ଏବେ ଦାସୀମାନେ ଲୋ ପଚାର ବେଗେ ଯାଇ ॥

Ekathā araji achhi caṇḍāluṇi muhin | Ebe dāsīmāne lo pacāra bege jāi ll

"This statement seems to be from a low-born person like me," she said. | "O maids, now go quickly and inquire properly."

ବ୍ରାହ୍ମଣ ହୋଇ ମୋ ଘରେ କି ରୂପେ ଖାଇବେ | ଚଣ୍ଡାଲୁଣୀ ଅନ୍ନ ଖାଇ ଅପବାଦ ନେବେ ॥

Brāhmaṇa hoi mo ghare ki rūpe khāibe | Caṇḍāluṇī anna khāi apabāda nebe ll

How can a Brahmin eat in my house? | If they eat food from a low-born woman (like me), they will receive defamation.

ଏ ମୋହର ଦ୍ରବ୍ୟ ତାଙ୍କୁ ଛୁଇଁ ନ ଯୋଗାଇ ।ଜାଣୁ ଜାଣୁ ମୁଁ କେମନ୍ତେ ପ୍ରକାରେ ଦେବଇଁ ॥

E mohara drabya tāṅku chuin na jogāi | Jāṇu jāṇu mun kemante prakāre debain ll

Let not my wealth touch them or be offered to them. | I wonder how I can even give it knowingly.

ଠାକୁରାଣୀ ସମୀପରୁ ଦାସୀମାନେ ଗଲେ | ବ୍ରାହ୍ମଣଙ୍କ ଆଗେ ଯାଇ ଏମନ୍ତ କହିଲେ ॥

Ṭhākurāṇī samīparu dāsīmāne gale | Brāhmaṇanka āge jāi emanta kahile ll

The maidservants left from the presence of the Goddess (Lakshmi). | They went before the Brahmins and told them this.

ଦାସୀଙ୍କ ମୁଖରୁ ଯେ ଏମନ୍ତ ବାକ୍ୟ ଶୁଣି | କ୍ଷୁଧାତୁର ହୋଇଣ କହନ୍ତ ହଳପାଣି ॥

Dāsīṅka mukharu je emanta bākya śuṇa | Kṣudhātura hoiṇa kahanta haḷapāṇi ll

Hearing such words from the maidservants... | Being extremely hungry, they replied in a feeble tone.

ନୂଆ ହାଣ୍ଡି ନୂଆସଞ୍ଚା ଦେଇ କି ପାରିବୁ । ଏମନ୍ତ ହୋଇଲେ ଆମ୍ଭେମାନେ ଯେ ଖାଇବୁ ॥

Nūā hāṇḍi nūāsañcā dei ki pāribu | Emanta hoile āmbhemāne je khāibu ॥

If you can give us new pots and new ladles, | If that is arranged, then we shall eat.

ଦାସୀମାନେ କହନ୍ତି ଲକ୍ଷ୍ମୀଙ୍କ ଆଗେ ଯାଇ । ହାତେ ରାନ୍ଧି ଭୋଜନ କରିବେ ଦୁଇଭାଇ ॥

Dāsīmāne kahanti Lakṣmīṅka āge jāi | Hāte rāndhi bhojana karibe duibhāi ॥

The maidservants went and spoke before Goddess Lakshmi, | That the two brothers will cook and eat with their own hands.

ଏହାଶୁଣି ମହାଲକ୍ଷ୍ମୀ ସନ୍ତୋଷ ହୋଇଲେ । ଦାସୀଙ୍କ ହସ୍ତରେ ହାଣ୍ଡି ଦଶଗୋଟି ଦେଲେ ॥

Ehāśuṇi Mahālaksmī santoṣa hoile | Dāsīmanka hastare hāṇḍi daśagoṭi dele ॥

Hearing this, Mahalakshmi became pleased, | And gave ten pots into the hands of the maidservants.

ଚାଉଳ ପଉଟିଏ ନେଇ ଛାମୁରେ ରଖିଲେ । ଲେଉଟିଆ ଶାଗ ନେଇ ପୁଳାଏକ ଦେଲେ ॥

Cāuḷa pa'uṭie nei chāmure rakhile | Leuṭiā śāga nei puḷāeka dele ll

She took a sack of rice and placed it on a winnowing fan. | She took tender leafy greens and gave a bundle of them.

ଆଳୁ ସାରୁ କଦଳୀ ଯେ ବଡ଼ି ବାଇଗଣ । ଦୁଧ ଦହି ଛେନା ଯେ ଶର୍କରୀ ଦେଲେ ପୁଣ ॥

Āḷu sāru kadaḷī je baḍi bāigaṇa | Dudha dahi chenā je śarkarī dele puṇa ll

Potatoes, colocasia, bananas, dried lentil dumplings, and eggplants— | Milk, curd, chhena (fresh cheese), and sugar were also given.

ଏବେ ଯେତେ ଇଛା ତେତେ ଭୁଞ୍ଜ ହୋ ବୋଇଲେ । ଗୃହେ ମହାଲକ୍ଷ୍ମୀ ଥାଇ ବିଚାର ଯେ କଲେ ॥

Ebe jete ichā tete bhuñja ho boile | Gṛuhe Mahālakṣmī thāi bicāra je kale ll

She said: "Now eat as much as you desire." | And Mahalakshmi, staying in the house, reflected (upon it).

ରାନ୍ଧଣା ଭୁଞ୍ଜିବେ ଯଦି ହାତେ ଦୁଇଭାଇ । ନାରୀଙ୍କୁ ପୁରୁଷ ଆଉ ଲୋଡ଼ିବେ କିମ୍ପାଇଁ ॥

Rāndhaṇā bhuñjibe jadi hāte duibhāi | Nārīṅku puruṣa āu loḍibe kimpāin ll

If the two brothers cook and eat with their own hands, | Then why would men need (or rely upon) women anymore?

ଲକ୍ଷ୍ମୀଦେବୀ କାଠଖଣ୍ଡେ ହସ୍ତରେ ଧଇଲେ । ଅଗ୍ନିର ସ୍ତମ୍ଭନ ମନ୍ତ୍ର ଦେବୀ ପାଠ କଲେ ॥

Lakṣmīdevī kāṭhakaṇḍe hastare dhaile | Agnira stambana mantra Devī pāṭha kale ll

Goddess Lakshmi held a piece of firewood in her hand, | And recited the fire-suppressing mantra (to stop the fire).

କଦାପି ଅଗ୍ନି ଦେବତା ତେଜ ନ ହୋଇବ | ହାଣ୍ଡି ନ ତାତିବ ଆଉ ପାଣି ନ ତାତିବ ॥

Kadāpi agni devatā teja na hoiba | Hāṇḍi na tātiba āu pāṇi na tātiba ll

From then on, the fire God would not produce heat, | Neither would the cooking pot heat up nor the water boil.

ଯେତେକାଠ ଜଳୁଥିବ ଭସ୍ମ ହୋଇଯିବ । କୁହୁଳି କରିଣ ତହୁଁ ଧୂଆଁ ହେଉଥିବ ॥

Jetekāṭha jaḷuthiba bhasma hoiyijiba | Kuhuḷi kariṇa tahun dhūān heuthiba ll

All the burning wood would turn into ashes, | And only smoke would come out, rising and swirling.

ଏମନ୍ତ ବୋଲିଣ କମଳା ଆଜ୍ଞା ଦେଲେ । ସେହି ପ୍ରକାରେଣ ଅଗ୍ନି ଦେବତା ଯେ କଲେ ॥

Emanta boliṇa kamaḷā ājñā dele | Sehi prakāreṇa agni devatā je kale ll

Thus saying, Kamala (another name for Lakshmi) gave her command, | And accordingly, the fire God acted as she said.

ସବୁ କାଠଯାକ ତହିଁ ଅଙ୍ଗାର ହୋଇଲା | ତେବେ ସୁଦ୍ଧା ଯେ କିଞ୍ଚିତେ ପାଣି ନ ତାତିଲା ॥

Sabu kāṭhajāka tahin aṅgāra hoilā | Tebe suddhā je kiñcite pāṇi na tātilā ll

All the collected firewood there turned into embers, | Yet still, not even a little water got warm.

ହଟି କମଳିନୀ ହଟ ଭିଆଇଲେ ଯେଣୁ । ହାଣ୍ଡିତଳେ କଳାଟିକେ ନ ପଡ଼ିଲା ତେଣୁ ॥

Haṭi Kamaḷinī haṭa bhiāile jeṇu | Hāṇḍitaḷe kaḷāṭike na paḍilā teṇu ll

As Kamalini (Lakshmi) withdrew and left, the kitchen seemed drenched (with failure), | Not even a speck of black soot formed under the cooking pot.

ସୁଗନ୍ଧ ତଇଳ ଦେବୀ ଦେଲେ ପଠିଆଇ । ଦାସୀମାନେ କହୁଛନ୍ତି ବ୍ରାହ୍ମଣଙ୍କୁ ଚାହିଁ ॥

Sugandha taila Devī dele paṭhiāi | Dāsīmāne kahuchhanti brāhmaṇanku cāhin ll

The Goddess sent fragrant oil (for bathing), | The maidservants asked the Brahmins, looking toward them (with care).

ପାକସିଦ୍ଧି ହେଲା କି ନୋହିଲା ହେ ଗୋସାଇଁ । ତଇଳ ଲଗାଇ ସ୍ନାନକର ବେଗେ ଯାଇଁ ॥

Pākasiddhi helā ki nohilā he gosāin | Taila lagāi snānkara bege jāin ll

"Has the cooking been completed or not, O Lords?" | "Apply the oil and go quickly for your bath."

ଜଗନ୍ନାଥ କହୁଛନ୍ତି ପାଣି ନ ତାତିଲା । କି ପାକ କରିବୁ ବେଳ ଉଛୁର ହୋଇଲା ॥

Jagannātha kahuchhanti pāṇi na tātilā | Ki pāka karibu beḷa uchura hoilā ll

Jagannath says, "The water hasn't heated up." | "How can we cook now? The time has passed."

ବଳରାମ କହୁଛନ୍ତି ଶୁଣରେ କହ୍ନାଇ । ଅନ୍ନ ହୋଇଲାକି ନାହିଁ କହ ବେଗେ ତୁହି ॥

Baḷarāma kahuchhanti śuṇare kahnā'i | Anna hoilāki nāhin kaha bege tuhi ll

Balram says, "Listen, dear brother...Kanhai (Krishna)," | "Tell me quickly — has the rice been cooked or not?"

ଜଗନ୍ନାଥ କହୁଛନ୍ତି ଶୁଣ ଆହେ ଭାଇ । ଅନ୍ନ କି ହୋଇବ ଟିକେ ପାଣି ତାତି ନାହିଁ ॥

Jagannātha kahuchhanti śuṇa āhe bhāi | Anna ki hoiba ṭike pāṇi tāti nāhin ll

Jagannath says, "Listen, oh brother," | "How will the rice be cooked? Not even a little water has heated up."

ବଳରାମ କହୁଛନ୍ତି ରେ ଅଧୁଆ ମୁହାଁ । ରାନ୍ଧି ନ ଜାଣି ହୋଇଅଛୁ ରାନ୍ଧୁଣିଆ ॥

Baḷarāma kahuchhanti re adhuā muhān | Rāndhi na jāṇi hoiachhu rāndhuṇiā ll

Balram says, "Hey unwashed-face (a slang implying incompetence)," | "You've become a cook without knowing how to cook."

ତୁହି ଆଢ଼ହୁଅ ମୁହିଁ ରାନ୍ଧୁଅଛି ଯାଇଁ। ଅନ୍ନ ରାନ୍ଧିବାକୁ ଗଲେ ବ୍ରାହ୍ମଣ ଗୋସାଇଁ ॥

Tuhi āḍhu'a muhin rāndhu'achi jāin | Anna rāndhibāku gale brāhmaṇa gosāin ll

"You step aside — I will go cook now." | So Lord Baḷarām *went to cook the rice.*

ଫୁଙ୍କି ଫୁଙ୍କି ବଳରାମ ବିରକ୍ତ ହୋଇଲେ । କାଠଖଣ୍ଡେ ଘେନିଣ ଯେ ହାଣ୍ଡି ପିଟିଦେଲେ ॥

Phuṅki phuṅki Baḷarāma birakta hoile | Kāṭhakaṇḍe gheniṇa je hāṇḍi piṭidele ll

Blowing and fanning the fire, Balram became irritated. | Grabbing a piece of firewood, he struck the pot in frustration.

କ୍ଷୁଧାରେ ଦୁଇଭାଇ ଆକୁଳ ହୋଇଲେ । କି ବୁଦ୍ଧି କରିବା ଜଗନ୍ନାଥଙ୍କୁ ବୋଇଲେ ॥

Kṣudhāre duibhāi ākula hoile | Ki buddhi karibā Jagannāthanku boile ||

The two brothers became distressed due to hunger. | "What should we do?" — they said to Jagannath.

ଜଗନ୍ନାଥ ବୋଇଲେ ତ ବୁଦ୍ଧ ଦିଶୁ ନାହିଁ । କ୍ଷୁଧାରେ ଆତୁର ହେଉଅଛି ମୋର ଦେହୀ ॥

Jagannātha boile ta buddha disu nāhin | Kṣudhāre ātura heuachi mora dehī ||

Jagannath said, "I see no solution (no idea comes to mind)." | "My body is tormented by hunger."

ବଳରାମ କହୁଛନ୍ତି ଶୁଣ ଜଗନ୍ନାଥ । ଜାତିପଛେ ଯାଉ ତାର ଘାରେ ଖାଉଁ ଭାତ ॥

Baḷarāma kahuchhanti śuṇa Jagannātha | Jātipache jāu tāra ghāre khāun bhāta ||

Balram says, "Listen, Jagannath," | "Forget caste — let's go and eat rice at this house."

ଯେବେ ଏହାଘରୁ ଭାତ ଆମ୍ଭଙ୍କୁ ନ ଦେବ । ଆମ୍ଭ ଦୁଇ ଭାଇଙ୍କର ମରଣ ହୋଇବ ॥

Jebe ehā-gharū bhāta āmbhaṅku na deba । Āmbha du'i bhāiṅkara maraṇa hoiba ॥

If from this house rice is not given to us, | Then we two brothers will die.

ଲେଉଟିଣ ଦାସୀ ଯାଇ ଲକ୍ଷ୍ମୀଙ୍କୁ କହିଲେ । ବ୍ରାହ୍ମଣ ତ ହାଣ୍ଡି ଭାଙ୍ଗି ଫୋପାଡ଼ଇ ଦେଲେ ॥

Leuṭiṇa dāsī jāi Lakṣmīṅku kahile । Brāhmaṇa ta hāṇḍi bhāṅgi phopāḍai dele ॥

The returning maid went and told Lakshmi, | "The Brahmins broke the cooking pot and burst out crying."

ଏହାଶୁଣି ମହାଲକ୍ଷ୍ମୀ ମନେ ଚିନ୍ତା କଲେ । କେତେ ଦୁଃଖ ଦୀନବନ୍ଧୁ ଦୁହେଁ ଯେ ପାଇଲେ ॥

Ehāśuṇi Mahālakṣmī mane cintā kale । Kete duḥkha dīnabandhu duheṅ je pāile ॥

Hearing this, Mahalakshmi became thoughtful (worried in her mind). | "How much sorrow these two protectors of the poor have endured."

ସୁବର୍ଣ୍ଣର ଚଟୁ ଗୋଟି ହସ୍ତରେ ଧଇଲେ | ରୋଷେଇ ଶାଳାକୁ ଲକ୍ଷ୍ମୀ ନିଜେ ବିଜେ କଲେ ॥

Suvarṇara caṭu goṭi hastare dhailā । Roṣei śāḷāku Lakṣmī nije bije kale ॥

She held a golden platter in her hand, | Lakshmi herself entered the kitchen.

ପ୍ରଥମେ ରାନ୍ଧିଲେ ମାଏ ବଗଡ଼ା ଯେ ଅନ୍ନ । ମୁଗ ମଧୁରୁଚି କ୍ଷୀର ନାନାଦି ବ୍ୟଞ୍ଜନ ॥

Prathame rāndhile mā'e bagaḍā je anna । Muga madhuruci kṣīra nānādi vyañcana ॥

First, the Mother cooked soft (steamed) rice, | Moong dal, sweet-flavoured kheer (rice pudding), and various other dishes.

ଆମ୍ବିଳ ଶାକର କଲେ କଦଳୀର ଭଜା | ଅତି ଯତ୍ନେ କଲେ ମାଏ ତିଅଣ ଯେ ମଞ୍ଜା ॥

Āmbiḷa śākara kale kadaḷīra bhajā । Ati jatne kale mā'e tiaṇa je mañjā ॥

She prepared sour leafy curry and fried banana. | With great care, the Mother made the special dish called Manja.

ଷାଠିଏ ପଉଟି ସେ ରନ୍ଧନ କଲେ ଯାଇ | ବଗଡ଼ା ଭାତ ମହିମା କଳନା ନ ଯାଇ ॥

Ṣāṭhi'e pauṭi se randhana kale jāi I Bagaḍā bhāta mahimā kalanā na jāi II

Sixty pauṭi (unit of measurement) of cooked rice packets she prepared one by one. | The glory of the soft rice is beyond imagination.

ଦୁଧପୁଳି କଲେ ମାତ ଘୃତପୁଳି କଲେ | ଅତି ଯତନରେ ମାଏ ସରପୁଳି କଲେ ॥

Dudhapuli kale māta ghṛutapuli kale I Ati jatanare mā'e sarapuli kale II

The mother prepared milk-filled sweet dumplings and ghee-fried dumplings. | With great effort, she made syrup-dipped pancakes (Sarapuli).

ଯେତେ ଦ୍ରବ୍ୟ ରାନ୍ଧିଛନ୍ତି ବ୍ରାହ୍ମଣଙ୍କ ରୁଚି । ବଡ଼ିର ମହୁର କଲେ ପକାଇଣ ସାଚି ॥

Jete drabya rāndhichanti brāhmaṇaṅka ruci I Baḍira mahura kale pakāiṇa sāci II

Whatever dishes were cooked, were all according to the Brahmins' taste. | She prepared a curry from dried lentil dumplings (badi) and seasoned it with care.

ସହସ୍ର ଆଟିକା ରାନ୍ଧି ଦ୍ରବ୍ୟ ସଜାଡ଼ିଲେ | ଯେ ଯାହା ସ୍ଥାନରେ ଯତ୍ନେ ରଖାଇଣ ଦେଲେ ॥

Sahasra āṭikā rāndhi drabya sajāḍile I Je jāhā sthānare jatne rakhāiṇa dele II

She cooked a thousand varieties and beautifully arranged the dishes. | Each item was placed thoughtfully in its designated spot.

କର୍ପୂର ଛେନା ଶର୍କରା ମରିଚ ଗୋଳାଇ | ଷାଠିଏ ନଉତି ପଣା ରଖିଲେ ତ ତହିଁ ॥

Karpūra chenā śarkarā marica goḷāi I Ṣāṭhi'e nauti paṇā rakhile ta tahin II

Camphor, chhena (curdled milk), sugar, and pepper were mixed and shaped into balls. | Sixty different ritual offerings (nauti pana) were arranged there.

ରଙ୍ଗବାଣ ପଇଡ଼ ସାଙ୍ଗରେ ଛେନାପଣା | ଅଦା ମିଶା କରି ଯେ ନବାତ ଖଣ୍ଡଛେନା ॥

Raṅgabāṇa paiḍa sāṅgare chenāpaṇā I Adā miśā kari je nabāta khaṇḍachenā II

Coloured, decorated betel leaves with chhena-based sweets were placed together. | Ginger was mixed into crystalline sugar and khanda chhena (a specific sweet).

ଲକ୍ଷ୍ମୀଙ୍କର ପାକ ଗୁଣ କେ କହି ପାରିବ | କ୍ଷଣକ ମଧରେ ମାଏ ସଜାଡ଼ିଲେ ସର୍ବ ॥

Lakṣmīṅkara pāka guṇa ke kahi pāriba I Kṣaṇaka madhyare Mā'e sajāḍile sarba II

Who can describe the excellence of Lakshmi's cooking? | Within moments, the mother arranged everything.

ସବୁଥିରୁ ଖଣ୍ଡିଏ ଖଣ୍ଡିଏ ରଖିଥିଲେ । ଭୋଜନ ଶେଷକୁ ପୋଡ଼ପିଠାଏ ରଖିଲେ ॥

Sabuthiru khaṇḍi'e khaṇḍi'e rakhithile I Bhojana śeṣaku poḍapiṭhāe rakhile II

A portion from each dish was set aside (as an offering or sample). | At the end of the meal, she placed Poda Pitha (a baked rice cake).

ବୋଇଲେ ଦାସୀଙ୍କି କର ଅଙ୍ଗ ମରଦନ । ବ୍ରାହ୍ମଣ ବୋଲିଣ ମନେ ନ ପାଞ୍ଚିବ ଭିନ୍ନ ॥

Boile dāsīnki kara aṅga maradana I Brāhmaṇa boliṇa mane na pāñciba bhinna II

She instructed the maidservants to massage the limbs (of the guests). | Saying "They are Brahmins," let no one treat them differently in mind.

ବ୍ରାହ୍ମଣମାନଙ୍କ ମୁହିଁ ଅଟେ ନିଜ ଦାସୀ । ଶୁଣିଣ ଆନନ୍ଦେ ଚଳିଗଲେ ସବୁ ଦାସୀ ॥

Brāhmaṇamānaṅka muhiṅ aṭe nija dāsī I Śuṇiṇa ānande caligale sabu dāsī II

I am the personal maid of the Brahmins (who serve them). | Hearing this, all the maidservants went joyfully.

ଦାସୀମାନେ କହୁଛନ୍ତି ସୁବେଦୀ ଗୋସାଇଁ । ସ୍ନାନକର ବେଗେ ଅଙ୍ଗ ମରଦନ ହୋଇ ॥

Dāsīmāne kahuchanti subedī gosāiṅ I Snānakara bege aṅga maradana hoi II

The maidservants say, "O learned Brahmin Lords," | "Quickly take bath by massaging your bodies properly."

ତହୁଁ ସୁବାସ ଜଳରେ ଦୁହେଁ ସ୍ନାନକଲେ । ଅଙ୍ଗ ପୋଛିବାକୁ ଦାସୀ ଗାମୁଛାଏ ଦେଲେ ॥

Tahuṅ subāsa jalare duheṅ snāna kale I Aṅga pochhibāku dāsī gāmućhāe dele II

Thereupon, the two (brothers) bathed in fragrant water. | To wipe their bodies, the maids gave them clean towels.

ପିନ୍ଧିବାକୁ ପିତାମ୍ବର ପାଟ ଆଣି ଦେଲେ । ସୁବେଶ ହୋଇଣ ଦୁଇ ଭାଇ ଯେ ବସିଲେ ॥

Pindhibāku pitāmbara pāṭa āṇi dele I Subeśa hoiṇa dui bhāi je basile II

For wearing, they brought silk yellow garments (Pitambara). | Dressed in fine attire, the two brothers sat down.

ବଳରାମ କହୁଛନ୍ତି ଶୁଣରେ କହ୍ନାଇ । ଏମନ୍ତ ପ୍ରକାରେ ମାନ୍ୟ କରେ କିସପାଇଁ ॥

Balarāma kahuchanti śuṇare Kahnāi I Emanta prakāre mānya kare kisapāin II

Balaram says, "Listen, dear Kanhai (Krishna)," | "Why are they honouring us in this way?"

ଏହାଘରେ ପୁରୁଷ ତ ଜଣେ ଦିଶୁନାହିଁ । ଶୂଳି ଦେବା ପ୍ରାୟେ ଏହି ବିଚାର ଦିଶଇ ॥

Ehā-ghare puruṣa ta jaṇe diśunāhin I Śūḷi debā prāye ehi bicāra diśai II

Not a single man is seen in this house. | This situation seems nearly worthy of being impaled (like a grave mistake or danger).

ଚାଲ ଏବେ ପଳାଇଣ ଏହିଠାରୁ ଯିବା । କ୍ଷଣକ ମଧ୍ୟରେ ଆଉ ପ୍ରାଣ ନ ପାଇବା ॥

Cāla ebe paḷāiṇa ehithāru jibā । Kṣaṇaka madhyare āu prāṇa na pāibā ॥

Come, let's escape and leave this place now. | In just a moment, we might lose our lives.

ଜଗନ୍ନାଥ କହୁଛନ୍ତି ଜ୍ୟେଷ୍ଠଭାଇ ଶୁଣ । ଏ ଘରର କର୍ତ୍ତା ଆଜ ହୋଇବେ ଆପଣ ॥

Jagannātha kahuchanti jyeṣṭhabhāi śuṇa । E gharara kartā āja hoibe āpaṇa ॥

Jagannath says, "Listen, elder brother," | You will be the master of this house today.

ବଳରାମ କହୁଛନ୍ତି ଶୁଣରେ କହ୍ନାଇ । ଏମନ୍ତ କହିବା ତୋର ଉଚିତ ନୁହଇ ॥

Balarāma kahuchanti śuṇare Kahnāi । Emanta kahibā tora ucita nuhai ॥

Balaram says, "Listen, dear Kanhai (Krishna)," | It is not proper for you to say such things.

ଗୃହ ପରିଷ୍କାର ଦେବୀ ସ୍ୱହସ୍ତରେ କଲେ । ଗନ୍ଧ ଚନ୍ଦନ ଯେ ମାଏ ଛଡ଼ା ଷକାଇଲେ ॥

Gṛuha pariṣkāra Devī svahastare kale I Gandha candana je Mā'e chaḍā ṣakāile II

The Goddess herself cleaned the house with her own hands. | She (the Mother Goddess) sprinkled fragrant sandalwood water and purified it.

ସୁବର୍ଣ୍ଣର ଥାଳି ସୁବର୍ଣ୍ଣର ଗିନାଝରି । ହାତଧୂଆ ପାଦଧୂଆ ସୁସଜ୍ଜିତ କରି ॥

Suvarṇara thāḷi suvarṇara ginājhari I Hātadhu'ā pādadhu'ā susajjita kari II

Golden plate, golden drinking vessel (goblet). | Hand-washing and foot-washing were arranged (made ready) beautifully.

ମଣୋହି କରିବା ବିଧି ଯେମନ୍ତେ ଭିଆଣ । ସୁବର୍ଣ୍ଣର ପୀଠ ତହିଁ କଲେକ ନିର୍ମାଣ ॥

Maṇohi karibā vidhi jemante bhiāṇa I Suvarṇara pīṭha tahin kaleka nirmāṇa II

As if to perform a beautiful marriage ritual (welcoming the groom with charm). | A golden seat (stool/platform) was constructed with artistic design.

ମହାଲକ୍ଷ୍ମୀ କହୁଛନ୍ତି ଦାସୀ ମୁଖ ଚାହିଁ । ବେଗ କରି ପ୍ରଭୁଙ୍କୁ ଲୋ ଘେନିଆସ ଯାଇ ॥

Mahālakṣmī kahuchanti dāsī mukha cāhin I Bega kari prabhuṅku lo gheniāsa jāi II

Mahalakshmi speaks, looking toward the maidservants, | "Quickly go and bring the Lords here."

ଏହାଶୁଣି ଦାସୀମାନେ ବେଗେ ଚଳିଗଲେ । ବ୍ରାହ୍ମଣଙ୍କ ପାଶେ ଯାଇଁ ପ୍ରବେଶ ହୋଇଲେ ॥

Ehāśuṇi dāsīmāne bege caligale I Brāhmaṇaṅka pāśe jāin prabeśa hoile II

Hearing this, the maidservants quickly went away. | They approached the Brahmins and entered near them.

ବିନୟରେ କହୁଛନ୍ତି ବ୍ରାହ୍ମଣ ଗୋସାଇଁ । ଭୋଜନ କରିବ ଚାଲ ସ୍ଥାନ ଅଛି ହୋଇ ॥

Binayare kahuchanti brāhmaṇa gosāin I Bhojana kariba cāla sthāna achi hoi II

With humility, they said, "O Brahmin Lords...", | "...Come to have the meal; the place is ready."

ବଳରାମ କହୁଛନ୍ତି ଶୁଣରେ କହ୍ନାଇ । ନାରୀଏ ଜଣେ ପୁରୁଷ କେହି ଏଥି ନାହିଁ ॥

Baḷarāma kahuchanti śuṇare kahanāi I Nārī'e jaṇe puruṣa kehi ethi nāhi II

Balaram says, "Listen, dear Kanhai (Krishna)," | Only women are here; there is no man in this house.

ଭିତରକୁ ଯିବା ଆମ୍ଭ ଉଚିତ ନୁହଁଇ । ପତ୍ର ଦୁଇଖଣ୍ଡ ତୁମ୍ଭେ ଆଣବେଗେ ଯାଇ ॥

Bhitaraku jibā ām̐bha ucita nuhai I Patra du'ikhaṇḍa tum̐bhe āṇabega jāi II

It is not proper for us to go inside. | You should quickly bring two leaf-plates.

ଜଗନ୍ନାଥ କହୁଛନ୍ତି ଶୁଣ ଭାଇ ତୁମ୍ଭେ | ଏ ଘରର କର୍ତ୍ତା ଆଜ ହୋଇବା ଯେ ଆମ୍ଭେ ॥

Jagannātha kahuchanti śuṇa bhāi tum̐bhe I E gharara karttā āja hoibā je ām̐bhe II

Jagannath says, "Listen, my brother," | Today, we shall be the masters (head) of this house.

କିମ୍ପା ତୁମ୍ଭେ ଭୟ କରୁଅଛ ଜ୍ୟେଷ୍ଠ ଭାଇ । ଦାତା ଦେଉଅଛି ଆମ୍ଭେ ଛାଡିବା କିମ୍ପାଇଁ ॥

Kimpā tum̐bhe bhaya karuchha jyeṣṭha bhāi I Dātā deŭachhi ām̐bhe chāḍibā kimpāin II

Why are you afraid, elder brother? | When the donor is giving, why should we reject it?

ଭୟେ ବଳରାମ ସେଠାବରୁ ନ ଉଠନ୍ତି । ହସ୍ତ ଧରି ଘେନିଗଲେ କମଳାଙ୍କ ପତି ॥

Bhaye Baḷarāma seṭhābaru na uṭhanti I Hasta dhari ghenigale Kamalāṅka pati II

Out of fear, Balaram did not rise from that place. | Holding his hand, Kamala's husband (Jagannath) took him along.

ଠାବ ସଞ୍ଚାରେ ଯେ ବଳରାମ ନ ବସନ୍ତି । ହସ୍ତଧରି ବସାଇଲେ ଦେବ ଶିରୀପତି ॥

Thāba sañcāre je Baḷarāma na basanti I Hasta dhari basāile Deba Sirīpati II

At the dining seat, Balaram was not sitting (reluctant to sit). | The Lord of Shri (Jagannath) made him sit by holding his hand.

କମଳିନୀ କହୁଛନ୍ତି ତୁଳସୀ ବ୍ରାହ୍ମଣୀ । ଦେଢ଼ଶୁର ମୋର ଯେ ଅଟନ୍ତି ହଳପାଣି ॥

Kamalinī kahuchanti Tulasī brāhmaṇī I Deḍhaśura mora je aṭanti Haḷapāṇī II

Kamala (Lakshmi) says to Tulasi, the Brahmin lady, | "Halapani (referring to Balaram) is my elder brother-in-law."

ତାହାଙ୍କୁ କେମନ୍ତେ ଅନ୍ନ ମୁହିଁ ଦେବି ନେଇ । ଭିତରେ ଥାଇଣ ମୁଁ ଯେ ଦେବଇଁ ବଢ଼ାଇ ॥

Tāhāṅku kemante anna muhin debi nei I Bhitare thāiṇa mun je debain baḍhāi II

How shall I personally give Him food? | Staying inside (the kitchen), I will serve it by extending (passing) it.

ବଡ଼ ସାନ ବୋଲି ଆଗ ପଚାରିବୁ ଯାଇ । ବଡ଼ଠାରେ ଆଗ ଅନ୍ନ ପରଶିବୁ ନେଇ ॥

Baḍa sāna boli āga pacāribu jāi I Baḍaṭhāre āga anna paraśiba nei II

Go and first ask who the elder and younger ones are. | To the elder, you will first serve food.

ଅନ୍ନଥାଳି ଘେନି ବେଗେ ବ୍ରାହ୍ମଣୀ ଅଇଲା । ବଡ଼ ସାନ କେଉଁ ପଣ୍ଡା ବୋଲି ପଚାରିଲା ॥

Annathāḷi gheni bege brāhmaṇī ailā । Baḍa sāna ke'un paṇḍā boli pacārilā ॥

Carrying a plate of rice, the Brahmin lady came quickly. | She asked, "Which among you is elder or younger, O Pandits?"

ବଳରାମ ବୋଲୁଛନ୍ତି ହୋଇଲୁକି କାଣୀ । ବଡ଼ ସାନ କିଏ ତୋତେ ନଦିଶଇ ପୁଣି ॥

Baḷarāma boluchanti hoiluki kāṇī । Baḍa sāna kie tote nadisai puṇi ॥

Balaram says, "Are you blind or what?" | "Can't you yourself see who is elder or younger?"

ଆମ୍ଭେ ବଡ଼ ବୋଲିଣ ଯେ ବଳରାମ କହି । ବ୍ରାହ୍ମଣୀ ବୋଇଲେ କୋପ କଲକି ଗୋସାଇଁ ॥

Ām̐bhe baḍa boliṇa je Baḷarāma kahi । Brāhmaṇī boile kopa kalaki gosāin ॥

"I am the elder," says Balaram. | The Brahmin lady said, "Did you get angry O Lord?"

ପ୍ରଥମ ଥାଳିର ଅନ୍ନ ବଳରାମେ ଦେଲା । ଭିତରକୁ ଆଉ ଅନ୍ନ ଆଣିବାକୁ ଗଲା ॥

Prathama thāḷira anna Baḷarāme delā I Bhitaraku āu anna āṇibāku galā II

She gave the first plate of rice to Balaram. | Then she went inside to bring more rice.

ଆଉ ଏକ ଥାଳି ଅନ୍ନ ଆଣିଲା ବେଳକୁ । ଚାରି ଗ୍ରାସରେ ଖାଇଲେ ବଳରାମ ତାକୁ ॥

Āu eka thāḷi anna āṇilā beḷaku I Cāri grāsare khāile Baḷarāma tāku II

She brought another plate of rice in due time. | Balaram ate that one in just four mouthfuls.

ଅନ୍ନ ଥାଳି ଘେନି କରି ବ୍ରାହ୍ମଣୀ ଅଇଲା । ଏ ପଣ୍ଡାର ଅନ୍ନଯାକ କିଏ ଘେନିଗଲା ॥

Anna thāḷi gheni kari brāhmaṇī ailā I E paṇḍāra annajāka kie ghenigalā II

Carrying the rice plate in her hand, the Brahmin lady came. | "Who took away this Pandit's rice portion?" she asked.

ବଳରାମ ବୋଇଲେ କ୍ଷୁଧାର୍ତ୍ତ ହୋଇଥିଲୁ । ଆଗକରି ଚାରିଗ୍ରାସ ବେଗେ ଖାଇଦେଲୁ ॥

Baḷarāma boile kṣudhārtto hoithilu । Āgakari cārigrāsa bege khāidelu ॥

Balaram said, "I was hungry." | "So I stepped ahead and quickly ate four mouthfuls."

ହସିଲା ବ୍ରାହ୍ମଣୀ ଦୁଇଭାଇଙ୍କୁ ଅନାଇଁ । କୁଟୁମ୍ବ ମାରିବା ପ୍ରାୟ ଦିଶୁଛ ଗୋସାଇଁ ॥

Hasilā brāhmaṇī du'ibhāiṅku anāin । Kuṭumba māribā prāya diśuchha gosāin ॥

The Brahmin lady laughed, looking at both the brothers. | "O Lord, you seem like someone who could fight over food with your own kin!"

ପୁତ୍ର ଭାରିଯା କି ତୁମ୍ଭ ଦୁହିଁଙ୍କର ନାହିଁ । ପେଟ ଲାଗି ବୁଲୁଅଛ ଦେଶ ଦେଶ ହୋଇ ॥

Putra bhārijā ki tum̐bha duhīṅkara nīhn । Peṭa lāgi bulůachha deśa deśa hoi ॥

"Have you two no sons or daughters to care for you?" | "You're roaming around country to country for your stomach's sake."

ସହସ୍ର କାନ୍ଦି କଦଳୀ ରଖିଦେଲେ ନେଇ । ଷାଠିଏ ନଉତି ପଣା ବେଗେ ଦେଲେ ଥୋଇ ॥

Sahasra kāndi kadaḷī rakhidele nei I Ṣāṭhi'e nauti paṇā bege dele thoi II

*She brought and placed a bunch of bananas weighing a thousand kāndīs (units). | She quickly placed sixty measures (*nauti*) of a dish (pāṇā) as an offering.*

ଯେଉଁପରି ପ୍ରଭୁଙ୍କର ମନକୁ ରୁଚଇ । ସେହିପରି କମଳିନୀ ଦିଅନ୍ତି ପଠାଇ ॥

Jeunpari prabhūṅkara manaku rucai I Sehipari Kamalinī dianti paṭhāi II

Just as the Lord's heart would be pleased (with certain things), | In the same way, Kamalini (Lakshmi) sent those very things to be given.

ଭୋଜନ ଶେଷକୁ ଯେ ବୋଲନ୍ତି ବଳରାମ । ଲକ୍ଷ୍ମୀଙ୍କ ରାନ୍ଧଣା ପରି ଲାଗୁଛି ଉତ୍ତମ ॥

Bhojana śeṣaku je bolanti Baḷarāma I Lakṣmīṅka rādhanā pari lāguchhi uttama II

At the end of the meal, Balaram said: | "This food seems as excellent as if cooked by Lakshmi herself."

ଜଗନ୍ନାଥ କହୁଛନ୍ତି ବଳଗାମ ଭାଇ । ଲକ୍ଷ୍ମୀପରା ଭାର୍ଯ୍ୟାକୁ ପାଇବା ଆଉ କାହିଁ ॥

Jagannātha kahuchanti Baḷarāma bhāi I Lakṣmīparā bhāryāku pāibā āu kāhin II

Jagannath said, "O Balaram brother," | "Where (else) can one get a Lakshmi-like wife again?"

ଲକ୍ଷ୍ମୀଙ୍କୁ ଭର୍ତ୍ସନା କରି ଦେଲେ ଘଉଡ଼ାଇ | ବାହାରି ଗଲେ ସେ ତାଙ୍କ ଇଚ୍ଛା ହେଲା ଯହିଁ ॥

Lakṣmīṅku bharṣanā kari dele gha'uḍāi I Bāhāri gale se tāṅka icchā helā jahin II

"We scolded Lakshmi and drove her away," | "She left and went wherever She wished."

ଏମନ୍ତ ସମୟେ ପୋଡ଼ପିଠା ଦେଲେ ନେଇ | ଜଗନ୍ନାଥ କହୁଛନ୍ତି ବଳରାମ ଭାଇ ॥

Emanta samaye poḍapiṭhā dele nei I Jagannātha kahuchanti Baḷarāma bhāi II

Just then, they were served the podapitha (roasted rice cake) and it was brought. | Jagannath said, "O Balaram brother!"

ମୋର ମନ କଥାକୁ ଯେ ଲକ୍ଷ୍ମୀ ଜାଣିଥାଇ । ଭୋଜନ ଶେଷକୁ ପୋଡ଼ପିଠାଏ ଦିଅଇ ॥

Mora mana kathāku je Lakṣmī jāṇithāi । Bhojana śeṣaku poḍapiṭhāe diai ॥

Lakshmi knows the feelings of my heart. | At the end of the meal, she gives podapitha (roasted rice cake).

ଭୋଜନ ସାରିଣ ପ୍ରଭୁ ଆଚମନ କଲେ । କର୍ପୂର ତାମ୍ବୁଳ ଦୁଇ ଭାଇ ଯେ ଭୁଞ୍ଜିଲେ ॥

Bhojana sāriṇa prabhu ācaman kale । Karpūra tāmbūla dui bhāi je bhuñjile ॥

After finishing the meal, the Lords performed achamana (ritual rinsing). | The two brothers chewed tambul (betel leaves) with camphor.

ବାହାର ମେଲାରେ ପ୍ରଭୁ ବିଜେକଲେ ଯାଇଁ । ଗବାକ୍ଷ ଦ୍ୱାରରେ ଲକ୍ଷ୍ମୀ ଅଛନ୍ତି ଅନାଇଁ ॥

Bāhāra melāre prabhu bijekale jāin । Gavākṣa dvārāre Lakṣmī achanti anāin ॥

The Lords stepped outside into the courtyard/fair after the meal. | Lakshmi is waiting at the window gate, quiet and unseen.

ପଚାର ପଚାର ଦାସୀ ପଚାରଲୋ ଯାଇ । ବିଭା ହୋଇଅଛନ୍ତି କି ପଣ୍ଡା ଦୁଇ ଭାଇ ॥

Pacāra pacāra dāsī pacāralo jāi I Bibhā hoiachanti ki paṇḍā dui bhāi II

Lakshmi said the maids, "Ask them, ask them repeatedly, going there:" | "Have the two Brahmin brothers gotten married?"

ଏହାଶୁଣି ଦାସୀମାନେ ବେଗେ ଚଳିଗଲେ । ବ୍ରାହ୍ମଣଙ୍କ ନିକଟରେ ପ୍ରବେଶ ହୋଇଲେ ॥

Ehāśuṇi dāsīmāne bege caligale I Brāhmaṇanka nikaṭare prabeśa hoile II

Hearing this, the maidservants quickly went. | They entered near the Brahmins.

ପୁତ୍ର ଭାରିଯା ଅଛି କି କାହିଁ ତୁମ୍ଭ ଘର | କେଉଁ ରାଜ୍ୟେ ବାଡ଼ି ବୃତ୍ତି ଶାସନ ତୁମ୍ଭର ॥

Putra bhārijā achi ki kāhin tumbha ghara I Keun rājyē bāḍi vṛutti śāsana tumbhara II

Do you have sons, wives, or what is your household like? | In which kingdom is your home? What is your occupation or rule?

ଜଗନ୍ନାଥ   କହୁଛନ୍ତି ଶୁଣ ଦାସୀ ତୁହି | ବିବାହ ହେବାକୁ ଦ୍ରବ୍ୟ ଆମ୍ଭର ଯେ ନାହିଁ ॥

Jagannātha kahuchanti śuṇa dāsī tuhi I Bibāha heba-ku drabya āmbhara je nāhin II

Jagannath says, "Listen, O maid..." | We don't have the means (wealth or items) to get married.

ଗୁଆବାଡ଼ି ଶାସନ ପାଇବୁ ଆମ୍ଭେ କାହିଁ | ଲକ୍ଷ୍ମୀପରା ଭାର୍ଯ୍ୟାକୁ ଯେ ଦେଲୁ ଘଉଡ଼ାଇ ॥

Guābāḍi śāsana pāibu āmbhe kāhin I Lakṣmīparā bhāryāku je delu gha'uḍāi II

How would we receive a kingdom like Guabadi to rule? | We offended Lakshmi, the noble wife, and drove Her out.

କପାଳମନ୍ଦ ଆମ୍ଭର ଦୁଇଭାଇ ବୁଲୁ । ଲକ୍ଷ୍ମୀ ଘଉଡ଼ାଇ ଆମ୍ଭେ ଏ ଦୁଃଖ ପାଇଲୁ ॥

Kapāḷamanda āmbhara duibhāi bùlu I Lakṣmī gha'uḍāi āmbhe e duḥkha pāilu II

We two brothers are ill-fated and wander aimlessly. | Lakshmi left in fury, and we have suffered this sorrow.

ଦାସୀଏ ବୋଇଲେ ପଣ୍ଡା ହୋଇଲ କି ବାଇ । ନାରୀକି ଛାଡ଼ି ପୁରୁଷ ଦରିଦ୍ର କି ହୋଇ ॥

Dāsīe boilē pandā hoila ki bāi I Nārī ki chāḍi puruṣa daridra ki hoi II

The maid said, "Have you lost your mind, O Panda?" | A man becomes poor if he is without a woman."

ଗୋବିନ୍ଦ ବୋଲନ୍ତି ଆମ୍ଭେ କହୁଅଛୁ ଶୁଣ । କେଉଁ ନାରୀ ଥିଲେ ହୁଏ ଐଶ୍ୱର୍ଯ୍ୟ ବର୍ଦ୍ଧନ ॥

Govinda bolanti āmbhe kahuachhu śuṇa I Keun nārī thilē hue aiśvarya bardhana II

Govinda (Lord Jagannath) says, "We are saying this, listen!" | Some women bring prosperity and increase in wealth.

କେଉଁନାରୀ ଥିଲେ ବଂଶ ନିପାତ ହୁଅଇ । କେଉଁ ନାରୀ ଥିଲେ ବାସୀ ପେଜ ନ ମିଳଇ ॥

Keun nārī thilē banśa nipāta hu'ai I Keun nārī thilē bāsī peja na miḷai II

Some women bring ruin to the entire lineage. | Because of some women, one can't even get stale rice water to drink.

କେଉଁ ନାରୀ ଥିଲେ ଶାଢ଼ୀ ସୁନା ବଳା ପାଇ । କେଉଁନାରୀ ଅଲକ୍ଷଣୀ ଗୃହକୁ ଭାଙ୍ଗଇ ॥

Keun nārī thilē sāḍhī sunā baḷā pāi I Keun nārī alakṣaṇī gṛuhaku bhāṅgai II

Some women cause men to gain fine clothes and gold bangles. | Some inauspicious women destroy the household.

ତୁମ୍ଭ ସାଆନ୍ତାଣୀଙ୍କୁ ଗୋ ପଚାର ତ ଯାଇ । ଦାସୀ କହେ ବାତୁଳ କି ହୋଇଲ ଗୋସାଇଁ ॥

Tumbha sāāntāṇınku go-pacāra ta jāi I Dāsī kahe bātula ki hoilā gosāin II

Go and ask your Queen (Saaantaṇī – Lakshmi). | The maid says, "O Lord, have you gone mad?"

କ୍ଷୁଧା ଲାଗୁଥିଲା ଏବେ ଭାତ ଯେ ଖାଇଲ । ଆମ୍ଭ ସାଆନ୍ତାଣୀଙ୍କୁ ଯେ ପଚରା ବୋଇଲ ॥

Kṣudhā lāguthilā ebe bhāta je khāila I Āmbhe sāāntāṇīnku je pacarā boila II

"Hunger was striking, You have eaten rice. " | "Now you ask us to ask our Queen (Saaantaṇī / Lakshmi)", the maid said.

ବଳରାମ ବୋଇଲେ ଏ ମୋର ପିଲାଭାଇ । ତୁମ୍ଭ ସାଆନ୍ତାଣୀ ଆଗେ ଜଣାଇବ ନାହିଁ ॥

Balarāma boile e mora pilābhāi I Tumbha sāāntāṇī āge jaṇāiba nāhin II

Balram said, "This is my younger brother..." | "You won't inform this to your Saaantaṇī (Lakshmi)",

ଜଗନ୍ନାଥ କହୁଛନ୍ତି ଭୟ କାହିଁପାଇଁ । କିଛି ନ ବିଚାର ଆହେ ବଳରାମ ଭାଇ ॥

Jagannātha kahuchanti bhaya kāhinpāi I Kichhi na bicāra āhe Balarāma bhāi II

Jagannath says, "Why be afraid?" | Don't think too much, O brother Balram.

ଲକ୍ଷ୍ମୀଙ୍କର ଗୃହ ସିନା ଅଟଇ ଯେ ଏହି । ଏଠାରେ ଆପଣ ଭୟ କର କିସପାଇଁ ॥

Lakṣmīṅkara gṛuha sinā aṭai je ehi I Eṭhāre āpaṇa bhaya kara kisapāin II

This is surely the inner home of Lakshmi. | Why are you yourself afraid here?

ବଳରାମ ବୋଲୁଛନ୍ତି ବାବୁ ଚକ୍ରଧର । ତୁମ୍ଭେ ଯାଇଁ ହସ୍ତଧର ମହାଲକ୍ଷ୍ମୀଙ୍କର ॥

Balarāma boluchanti bābu Cakradhara I Tumbhe jāi hastadhara Mahālakṣmīnkara II

Balram says, "O Chakradhara (wielder of the discus), dear brother..." | You go and take the hand of Mahalakshmi (to approach her).

ଆମ୍ଭେ ଦୋଷ କଲୁ ବୋଲି କହ ତାଙ୍କୁ ଯାଇ । ଯହିଁ ଇଚ୍ଛା ତହିଁ ଥାଅ ଆମ୍ଭ ମନା ନାହିଁ ॥

Āmbhe doṣa kalu boli kaha tāṅku jāi I Jahin icchā tahin thāa āmbha manā nāhin II

Go and tell her, "We have committed a fault." | Wherever she wishes to stay, let her be; we have no objection.

ଯେତେବେଳେ ବଳରାମ ଏମନ କହିଲେ | ଭିତର ପୁରକୁ ପ୍ରଭୁ ନିଜେ ବିଜେ କଲେ ॥

Jetebeḷe Balarāma emanta kahile I Bhitarapuraku prabhu nije bije kale II

When Balram spoke this way... | The Lord Himself entered the inner palace

ଧୀରେ ଧୀରେ ଭିତରକୁ ଗଲେ ପୀତବାସ । ପ୍ରବେଶ ହୋଇଲେ ଯାଇ କମଳାଙ୍କ ପାଶ ॥

Dhīre dhīre bhitaraku gale pītabāsa I Prabeśa hoile jāi Kamalāṅka pāśa II

Slowly, the one clad in yellow garments (Lord Jagannath) went inside... | He entered and went near Kamala (Goddess Lakshmi).

ପାଣିଝରି ଘେନିକରି କମଳା ଅଇଲେ । ଦରହାସେ ପ୍ରଭୁଙ୍କର ମୁଖକୁ ଚାହିଁଲେ ॥

Pāṇijhari ghenikari Kamalā aile I Darahāse prabhuṅkara mukhaku cāhile II

Kamala came carrying a water pot. | With a gentle smile, she looked at the Lord's face.

ଅତି ଯତନରେ ଦେଲେ ପାଦପଦ୍ମ ଧୋଇ । ଥୋପାଏ ପାଦ ଉଦକ ମସ୍ତକେ ଲଗାଇ ॥

Ati jatanare dele pādapadma dhoi I Thopāe pāda-udaka mastake lagāi II

With great care, she washed the lotus feet (of the Lord). | She sprinkled the foot-washing water on her own head.

କିଛି ପାଦୋଦକ ଲକ୍ଷ୍ମୀ ଗର୍ଭକୁ କ୍ଷେପିଲେ । ପଞ୍ଚବର୍ଣ୍ଣେ ପୁଷ୍ପେ ପାଦପଦ୍ମ ପୂଜାକଲେ ॥

Kichhi pādodaka Lakṣmī garbhaku kṣepile I Pañcabarṇe puṣpe pādapadma pūjakale II

Lakshmi sprinkled some foot-wash water into the sanctum (or inner chamber). | With five-colored flowers, she worshipped the lotus feet (of the Lord).

ମହାଲକ୍ଷ୍ମୀ କହୁଛନ୍ତି ପ୍ରଭୁଙ୍କୁ ଅନାଇ । ଚଣ୍ଡାଲୁଣୀ ବୋଲି ମୋତେ ଦେଲ ଘଉଡ଼ାଇ ॥

Mahālakṣmī kahuchanti prabhunku anāi I Caṇḍāluṇī boli mote dela gha'uḍāi II

Mahalakshmi said to the Lord with displeasure... | You drove me out saying I am a Chandāḷunī (outcaste woman).

ଚଣ୍ଡାଲୁଣୀ ଘରେ ଏବେ ଭୁଞ୍ଜିଲ ଗୋସାଇଁ । ଚଣ୍ଡାଳ ବିଟାଳ ହେଲ ଦୁଇଗୋଟି ଭାଇ ॥

Caṇḍāluṇī ghare ebe bhuñjila gosāin I Caṇḍāla biṭāla hela duigoṭi bhāi II

Now, my Lord, you have eaten in the house of a Chandāḷunī. | Both of you brothers have become Chandaḷas and degraded.

ଧିକ ତୁମ୍ଭ ବଡ଼ପଣ ଧିକ୍ ତୁମ କଥା । ପୋଡୁ ତୁମ୍ଭର ପ୍ରତିଜ୍ଞା ଧିକ୍ ତୁମ୍ଭ ଭ୍ରାତା ॥

Dhik tumbha baḍapaṇa dhik tuma kathā I Poḍu tumbhara pratijñā dhik tumbha bhrātā II

Shame on your greatness! Shame on your words! | Burn your vows! Shame on your brother!

ମହାଲକ୍ଷ୍ମୀ ଏ ପ୍ରକାରେ ବହୁ ଧିକାରିଲେ | କାଳୀୟ ଗଞ୍ଜନ ଶୁଣି କିଛି ନ କହିଲେ ॥

Mahālakṣmī e prakāre bahu dhikārile I Kāḷīya gañjana śuṇi kichhi na kahile II

Mahalakshmi thus continued to condemn (them) repeatedly. | Hearing such harsh scolding, the Lord said nothing.

ମହାମାୟୀ ବୋଇଲେ ହେ ଶୁଣ ମୋ ବଚନ | ମୋର କିସ କାର୍ଯ୍ୟ ତୁମ୍ଭେ କହ ହେ ବହନ ॥

Mahāmāyī boile he śuṇa mo bacana I Mora kisa kārya tumbhe kaha he bahana II

Mahāmāyī (the Great Enchantress) said: "O listen to my words," | "What is my duty? You tell me, O husband."

କିଛିକ୍ଷଣ ଉତ୍ତାରେ ବୋଇଲେ ଜଗନ୍ନାଥ । ଏବେ ମନୁ ମାନ ତେଜ ଜଗତର ମାତ ॥

Kichhikṣaṇa uttāre boile Jagannātha I Ebe manu māna teja jagatara mātha II

After a moment, Jagannātha replied: | "Now calm your mind, O radiant Mother of the world."

ଅକାରଣେ ଏତେ କଥା କହ ପ୍ରାଣସହୀ । ଆମ୍ଭର ପ୍ରାର୍ଥନା ଆମ୍ଭସଙ୍ଗେ ଯିବାପାଇଁ ॥

Akāraṇe ete kathā kaha prāṇasahī I Āmbhara prārthanā āmbhasaṅge jibāpāin II

"Why do you speak so many words without reason, beloved?" | "We request you to accompany us."

ବଡ଼ହେଲେ କିସ ହେଲା ଗରବ ଗଞ୍ଜିଲ । ରବିତଳେ ସବୁ ଯୁଗେ ଯଶ ରଖିଗଲ ॥

Baḍa hele kisa helā garaba gañjila I Ravitaḷe sabu juge jaśa rakhigala II

"What is the use of greatness if pride destroys it?" | "Beneath the Sun, the glory is upheld through all ages.."

ତୁମ୍ଭ ଯୋଗେ ଆମ୍ଭେ କଷ୍ଟ ପାଇଲୁ ବହୁତ । ଆମ୍ଭେ ଭିକ୍ଷା ମାଗିବାର ଜାଣିଲେ ଜଗତ ॥

Tumbha joge āmbhe kaṣṭa pāilu bahuta I Āmbhe bhikṣā māgibāra jāṇile jagata II

Because of you, we suffered a lot. | The world came to know that we begged for food.

ତୁମ୍ଭ ଯଶକୀର୍ତ୍ତି ଏବେ ଜଗତେ ରହିଲା । ଆମ୍ଭଙ୍କୁ ଅନ୍ନ ଦେବାର ଜଗତ ଶୁଣିଲା ॥

Tumbha jaśakīrtti ebe jagate rahilā I Āmbhanku anna debāra jagata śuṇilā II

Your fame and glory have now remained in the world. | The world heard that you gave us food.

ଗୁରୁବାର ଦିନ ଯେ ଏ ପୁରାଣ ଶୁଣିବ । ଜନ୍ମ ଜନ୍ମାନ୍ତର ପାପ ତାର କ୍ଷୟ ହେବ ॥

Gurubāra dina je epurāṇa śuṇiba I Janma janmāntara pāpa tāra kṣaya heba II

Whoever listens to this Purana on a Thursday, | Their sins of many lifetimes will be destroyed.

ଲକ୍ଷ୍ମୀପୂଜା ଦିନ ଏହା ଯେ ନାରୀ ଗାଇବ । ଇହ ଜନ୍ମେ ପତିବ୍ରତା ବୈକୁଣ୍ଠକୁ ଯିବ ॥

Lakṣmīpūjā dina ehā je nārī gāiba I Iha janme pativratā Vaikunthaku jiba II

A woman who sings this on the day of Lakshmi Puja, | Will be a devoted wife in this life and go to Vaikuntha (heavenly abode of Vishnu).

ଯଦ୍ୟପି କେହି ନାରୀକୁ ମୁଖେ ବୁଝାଇବ । ତାହାର ସୁକୃତ ଆଉକେ କହି ପାରିବ ॥

Jadyapi kehi nārīku mukhe bujhāiba I Tāhāra sukṛuta āuke kaha pāriba II

Even if someone explains it orally to a woman, | Who can truly describe the merit (virtue) of that person?

ଏତେ କହି ଗୋବିନ୍ଦ ଧଇଲେ ଲକ୍ଷ୍ମୀହସ୍ତ । ଜଗତ ମାତ ବୋଇଲେ କର ତୁମ୍ଭେ ସତ୍ୟ ॥

Ete kahi Govinda dhailē Lakṣmīhasta I Jagata māta boilē kara tumbhe satya II

Saying this much, Govinda (Jagannath) held Lakshmi's hand. | The Mother of the world (Lakshmi) said, "Now act truthfully and promise me."

ଚଣ୍ଡାଳୁ ବ୍ରାହ୍ମଣ ଯାଏ ଖୁଆଖୋଇ ହେବେ । ସମସ୍ତେ ଖାଇଣ ହସ୍ତ ଜଳେ ନ ଧୋଇବେ ॥

Caṇḍāḷu brāhmaṇa jāe khuākhoyi hebe । Samaste khāiṇa hasta jale na dhoibe ॥

The Caṇḍāla and the Brahmin will go and eat and drink together. | All will eat without washing their hands with water.

ହାଡ଼ିର ହସ୍ତୁ ବ୍ରାହ୍ମଣ ଛଡ଼ାଇ ଖାଇବେ । ବ୍ରାହ୍ମଣେ ଖାଇ ହସ୍ତକୁ ମୁଣ୍ଡରେ ପୋଛିବେ ॥

Hāḍira hastu brāhmaṇa chaḍāi khāibe । Brāhmaṇe khāi hastaku muṇḍare pochibe ॥

Brahmins will eat by taking food directly from the hands of the Hadis (low-caste). | After eating, the Brahmin will wipe his hand on his head.

ଅନ୍ନ ଖାଇ ସର୍ବେ ମୁଣ୍ଡେ ପୋଛୁଥିବେ ହସ୍ତ । ତେବେ ବଡ଼ ଦେଉଳକୁ ଯିବି ଜଗନ୍ନାଥ ॥

Anna khāi sarbe muṇḍe pocchuthibe hasta । Tebe baḍa deuḷaku jibi Jagannātha ॥

Everyone, after eating rice, will wipe their hands on their heads. | Then I will go back to the main temple (Bada Deula), O Jagannath.

ହେଉ ହେଉ ବୋଲି ଆଜ୍ଞା ଦେଲେ ମହାବାହୁ । ଯୁଗେ ଯୁଗେ ଲକ୍ଷ୍ମୀ ଗୋ ତୁମ୍ଭର ଯଶ ରହୁ ॥

Heu heu boli ājñā delē Mahābāhu I Juge juge Lakṣmī go tumbhara jaśa rahu II

"So be it, so be it," said the mighty-armed Lord (Jagannath). | O Lakshmi, may your fame remain through the ages.

ଲକ୍ଷ୍ମୀଙ୍କ ହସ୍ତ ଧରିଣ ଜଗନ୍ନାଥ ନେଲେ । ବଡ଼ ଦେଉଳକୁ ପ୍ରଭୁ ବିଜେ କରିଗଲେ ॥

Lakṣmīṅka hasta dhariṇa Jagannātha nele I Baḍa deuḷaku prabhu bije karigale II

Holding Lakshmi's hand, Jagannath took her along. | The Lord proceeded to re-enter the Great Temple (Bada Deula).

ଲକ୍ଷେ ଚନ୍ଦ୍ରଉଦିଆଯେ ଛାମୁରେ ଜଳଇ । ଦେଉଳକୁ ବିଜେକଲେ ବ୍ରହ୍ମାଣ୍ଡ ଗୋସାଇଁ ॥

Lakṣe candraudiyāje chāmure jala'i I Deuḷaku bije kale brahmāṇḍa Gosā'in II

Like the rising of a hundred thousand moons, the courtyard was shining (glowing). | The Lord of the Universe (Jagannath) entered the temple.

ଇନ୍ଦ୍ର ଡାକୁଛନ୍ତି ଦେବ ମଣିମା ମଣିମା । ବ୍ରହ୍ମା ଡାକୁଛନ୍ତି ଦେବ ଗୁହାରୀ ଶୁଣିମା ॥

Indra ḍākuchanti Deba Maṇimā Maṇimā I Brahmā ḍākuchanti Deba guhārī śuṇimā II

Indra was calling out, "Deva, Manima! Manima!" ("Manima" is a revered cry for the Lord, often heard in Puri.) | Brahma was calling, "O Lord, hear our prayers!"

ବରୁଣ କୁବେର ଯେ ହସରେ ବେତ ଧରି । ନୃତ୍ୟ କରୁଥିଲେ ଯହିଁ ସ୍ୱର୍ଗ ଅପସରି ॥

Baruṇa Kubera je hasare beta dhari I Nṛutya karuthile jahin svarga apsarī II

Varuna and Kubera were holding canes (staffs) in hand with joy, | Where heavenly nymphs (Apsaras) were dancing.

ରମ୍ଭା ଯେ ମେନକା ଆଦି ଆଉ ଚିତ୍ରଲେଖା । ତୁଳସୀ ମାଳତୀ ଆଉ ଅନ୍ୟାନ୍ୟ ରସିକା ॥

Rambhā je Menakā ādi āu Citralekhā I Tulāsī Mālatī āu anyānnya rasikā II

Rambha, Menaka, and also Chitralekha, | Tulasi, Malati, and other graceful charming women,

ଚଞ୍ଚଳା ଯେ ମଦାଳସୀ ଆବର ସୁଶୀଳା । ନୃତ୍ୟ ଆରମ୍ଭନ୍ତି ତୁଷ୍ଟ ହୋଇ ସେ ଅବଳା ॥

Cañcalā je Madāḷasī ābara suśīlā I Nṛutya ārambhanti tuṣṭa hoi se abalā II

Restless Madalasa and also the gentle ones (like Sushila), | All those women began to dance with joy and satisfaction.

ବଳରାମ କହୁଛନ୍ତି ଶୁଣରେ କହ୍ନାଇ । ଘରକୁ ଘରଣୀ ସିନା ସୁନ୍ଦର ଦିଶଇ ॥

Balarāma kahuchanti śuṇare Kahnā'i I Gharaku gharaṇī sinā sundara diśa'i II

Balaram says — listen, O Kanhai (Krishna). | The house looks truly beautiful when the housewife is present.

ଯେତେବେଳେ ଦାଣ୍ଡେ ଯାଉଥିଲୁ ଦୁଇଭାଇ । ଚୋର ଖଣ୍ଟ ବୋଲି ଦେଉଥିଲେ ଘଉଡ଼ାଇ ॥

Jetebele dāṇḍe jāuthilu duibhā'i I Cora khaṇṭa boli deutthile ghuḍā'i II

At the time when we, the two brothers, were walking along the street, | They scolded and drove us out calling "thieves and thugs."

ଆହୁରି କଥାଏ ଶୁଣ ଜଗନ୍ନାଥ ଭାଇ । ଲକ୍ଷ୍ମୀ ଏତେ ବଡ଼ ବୋଲି ଏବେ ଜାଣିଲଇଁ ॥

Āhuri kathāe śuṇa Jagannātha bhā'i I Lakṣmī ete baḍa boli ebe jāṇilain II

Listen further, brother Jagannath, | Only now we have realized how great Lakshmi truly is.

ଲକ୍ଷ୍ମୀ ଦେବୀ ବିଜେକଲେ ତାଙ୍କ ଦେଉଳକୁ । ଦୁଇଭାଇ ବିଜେ କଲେ ବଡ଼ ଦେଉଳକୁ ॥

Lakṣmī Debī bije kale tāṅka deuḷaku I Duibhā'i bije kale baḍa deuḷaku II

Goddess Lakshmi re-entered her temple (abode). | The two brothers also re-entered the main temple.

ଦାସୀ ପରିବାରୀ ଆଦିକରି ଯେତେ ଥିଲେ | ଲକ୍ଷ୍ମୀ ଆସିଲାରୁ ସେ ସମସ୍ତ ଯେ ଅଇଲେ ॥

Dāsī paribārī ādikari jete thile I Lakṣmī āsilāru se samasta je aile II

All the maidservants and attendants who had left earlier, | Returned as soon as Lakshmi arrived.

ଲକ୍ଷ୍ମୀଙ୍କୁ ପାଇଣ ଦେବ ଗୋବିନ୍ଦ ଆନନ୍ଦ । ସଂସାରରେ ସେହିମତେ କଲେକ ମୁକୁନ୍ଦ ॥

Lakṣmīṅku pāiṇa deba Govinda ānanda I Saṁsārare sehimate kaleka Mukunda II

Govinda (Krishna) became joyful upon being reunited with Lakshmi. | Mukunda (another name for Krishna) made the world similarly blissful.

ଶୁଣିଲେ ନାରଦ ଏହି ପୁରାତନ ଆଖ୍ୟା । ଯାହା ପ୍ରସନ୍ନରେ ପ୍ରଭୁ ମାଗିଲେ ଯେ ଭିକ୍ଷା ॥

Śuṇile Nārada ehi purātana ākhyā I Jāhā prasannare prabhu māgile je bhikṣā II

Narada heard this ancient narrative. | Wherein the Lord (Jagannath) had once begged alms in a pleased state.

ଛାର ଚଣ୍ଡାଳୁଣୀ ଅଇଶ୍ୱର୍ଯ୍ୟ ଭୋଗକଲା । ଲକ୍ଷ୍ମୀଙ୍କର ସୁଦୟାରେ ଏମନ୍ତ ହୋଇଲା ॥

Chāra caṇḍāḷuṇī aiśvarya bhogakalā I Lakṣmīṅkara sudayāre emanta hoilā II

Even an outcaste woman (Chandaluṇī) enjoyed great prosperity (opulence). | Such was made possible by the compassionate grace of Lakshmi.

ଏ ପୁରାଣ ପଢ଼ିଲେ ଯେ ସର୍ବସିଦ୍ଧି ହୁଏ । ସୂର୍ଯ୍ୟୋଦୟ ତମ ସମ ପାପ କ୍ଷୟ ଯାଏ ॥

E purāṇa paḍhile je sabasiddhi hue I Sūryodaye tama sama pāpa kṣaya jā'e II

Whoever reads this Purana attains all accomplishments (success). | As the sun rises, all sins vanish like darkness.

ଏ ପୁରାଣ ଯେଉଁମାନେ ପଢ଼ନ୍ତି ଶୁଣନ୍ତି । ଲକ୍ଷେ କୋଟି ଗୋଦାନରେ ଫଳ ଯେ ଲଭନ୍ତି ॥

E purāṇa jaunmāne paḍhanti śuṇanti I Lakṣe koṭi godānare phala je labhanti II

Those who read or listen to this Purana, | They attain the merit equal to donating lakhs of crores of cows.

ଏ ପୁରାଣ ଅଟଇ ଯେ ମୁକତିର ପଥ । ଏହାଫଳ କଥନରେ କେ ହେବ ସମର୍ଥ ॥

E purāṇa aṭa'i je muktira patha I Ehāphala kathanare ke heba samartha II

This Purana indeed is the path to liberation (moksha). | Who can be capable of describing the fruits (benefits) of it?

ଲକ୍ଷ୍ମୀଙ୍କ ପୁରାଣ ଏହୁ ସମ୍ପୂର୍ଣ୍ଣ ହୋଇଲା | ଭାବେ ବଳରାମ ଦାସ ଗୀତରେ କହିଲା ॥

Lakṣmīṅka purāṇa ehu sampūrṇa hoilā I Bhābe Balarāma Dāsa gītare kahilā II

This Purana of Lakshmi is now completed. | With devotion, Balaram Das narrated it through song.

।। ଇତି ଶ୍ରୀ ଲକ୍ଷ୍ମୀପୁର।ଣ ସମ୍ପୂର୍ଣ୍ଣ ।।

II Iti Śrī Lakṣmīpurāṇa sampūrṇa II

Thus ends the Śrī Lakṣhmi Purāṇa.

CHAPTER 2
THE MANTRAS

<u>ଶ୍ରୀ ଶ୍ରୀ ଲକ୍ଷ୍ମୀପୁରାଣ ସ୍ତବ</u>

<u>Śrī Śrī Lakṣmīpurāṇa Stava</u>

Revered Lakṣmī Purāṇa Hymn

ତ୍ରୈଲୋକ୍ୟ ପୂଜିତେ ଦେବା କମଳେ ବିଷ୍ଣୁ ବଲ୍ଲଭେ

Trailokya pūjite debā Kamale Vishnu vallabhe

O Goddess Kamala (Lakshmi), worshipped in all three worlds (heaven, earth, and underworld), beloved of Lord Vishnu.

ଯଥା ତ୍ୱଂ ସ୍ୱସ୍ଥିରା କୃଷ୍ଣେ ତଥା ଭବ ମହୀପରା ।

Yathā tvaṁ svasthirā kṛuṣṇe tathā bhaba mahīparā ।

Just as you remain steadfast with Lord Krishna, may you also dwell steadily in my home on earth.

ଈଶ୍ୱରୀ କମଳା ଲକ୍ଷ୍ମୀ ଚଞ୍ଚଳା ଶ୍ରୀ ହରିପ୍ରିୟା ପଦ୍ମ

Īśvarī Kamalā Lakṣmī cañcalā śrī Haripriyā Padma

Names of Goddess Lakshmi: Īśvarī (Supreme Lady), Kamalā (Lotus One), Lakṣmī (Wealth), Cañcalā (Fickle), Śrī (Prosperity), Haripriyā (Beloved of Hari/Vishnu), Padma (Lotus).

ପଦ୍ମାଳୟା ସଂପଦ ଶ୍ରୀ ପଦ୍ମ ଧାରିଣୀ

Padmālayā saṁpada śrī padma dhāriṇī ll

She who dwells in the lotus (Padmālayā), is the embodiment of wealth (Sampada), prosperity (Śrī), and bearer of the lotus (Padma Dhāriṇī).

ଦ୍ୱାଦଶୈତାନି ନାମାନି ଲକ୍ଷ୍ମୀ ସମ୍ପୂର୍ଣ୍ୟ ଯଃ ପଠେତ୍

Dvādaśaitāni nāmāni Lakṣmī sampūrṇya yaḥ paṭhet

Whoever recites these twelve names of Lakshmi completely...

ସ୍ଥିର ଲକ୍ଷ୍ମୀ ଭବେତ୍ତସ୍ୟ ପୁତ୍ର ଦାରାଭିତିଃ ସହ ।

Sthira Lakṣmī bhavet tasya putra dārābhitiḥ saha ll

...will be blessed with steady wealth (Sthira Lakshmi), along with sons, wife, and a stable household.

ଲକ୍ଷ୍ମୀଙ୍କ ଧ୍ୟାନ

Lakṣmīṅka Dhyāna

Lakshmi Dhyāna – Meditation on Goddess Lakshmi

ଓଁ ପାଶାକ୍ଷ ମାଳିକାମ୍ଭୋଜ ସ୍କ ରି ଭାର୍ଷ୍ୟମ୍ୟମ୍ୟମେ ସୈୟୋଃ ।

Oṁ pāśākṣa mālikāmbhoja skarī bhārṣyamyamyaṁ saiyoḥ I

Om. The Goddess who holds a noose (pāśa), a rosary (akṣamālā), and a lotus (ambhoja) in her hands (skari), whose form is charming and radiant, and who is seated on a lotus.

ପଦ୍ମାସନସ୍ଥାଂଧ୍ୟାୟେନ ତ୍ରୈ ଲୋ ।କ୍ୟ ମାତର ।ମା

Padmāsanasthāṁ dhyāyena trailokya mātaraṁ

I meditate on the Mother of the Three Worlds (trailokya-mātaram) who is seated on a lotus (padmāsana).

ଗୌରବର୍ଣ୍ଣାଂ ସ୍ୱରୂ ପାଞ୍ଚ

Gauravarṇāṁ svarūpāñca I

She is of fair complexion (gaura-varṇāṁ), and has a divine beautiful form (svarūpa).

ସର୍ବାଳଙ୍କାର ଭୂଷିତମ୍

Sarvālaṅkāra bhūṣitam

Adorned with all kinds of ornaments (sarva-alaṅkāra-bhūṣitam).

ରୌକପଦ୍ମ ବ୍ୟଗ୍ରବରଂ ବରହଂ ଦକ୍ଷିଣେନାତୁ ।

Raukpadma vyagravaraṁ varahaṁ dakṣiṇenātu ll

She displays a lotus (padma) and the boon-bestowing gesture (vara-mudrā) in her right hand (dakṣiṇa), and is ever ready to bless (vyagra = eager).

<u>ପୁଷ୍ପାଞ୍ଜଳୀ</u>

<u>Puṣpāñjali</u>

Pushpāñjali – Floral Offering

ନମସ୍ତେ ସର୍ବ ଦେବନାଂ

Namaste sarva devanāṁ

Salutations to you, O one revered by all the Gods.

ବରଦାସୀ ହରସପ୍ରିୟେ

Varadāsi Harasapriyē

O giver of boons (varadā), O beloved of Hara (Lord Vishnu).

ଗତିସ୍ତଂ ପ୍ରସନ୍ନାନାଂ

Gatistvaṁ prasannānāṁ

You are the refuge (gati) of those who are pleased or serene in mind.

ସାମଭୟାନ୍ମତ୍ତ୍ୱ ଦଳନଦ୍ ।

Sāmbhavyānmatva dalanad ll

You destroy ignorance (mattva) and fear (bhaya), especially of those devoted to the sāma (peace/harmony).

ପ୍ରଣାମ ମନ୍ତ୍ର

Praṇāma Mantra

Mantra of Salutation

ନମୋ ବିଶ୍ୱରୂପସ୍ୟ

Namo viśvarūpasya

Salutations to the One who has the form of the entire universe (Viśvarūpa).

ଭାର୍ଶ୍ୱର୍ଯ୍ୟାସି ପଦ୍ମ

Bhārṣvaryyāsi padma

Who is adorned with a lotus, or who has the lotus as her seat (padma = lotus; bhārṣvaryyāsi = poetic compound, interpreted as "you who are radiant/glorious").

ପଦ୍ମାଳୟେ ଶୁଭେ

Padmālaye śubhe

O auspicious One who resides in the lotus (Padmālayā = abode of the lotus).

ସର୍ବତ୍ର ପାହି ମାଂ

Sarvatra pāhi māṁ

Protect me everywhere (sarvatra = everywhere, pāhi = protect, māṁ = me).

ମାତଃ ଲକ୍ଷ୍ମୀଦେବୀ ନମୋସ୍ତୁତେ ।

Mātaḥ Lakṣmīdevī namostute ll

O Mother Lakshmi, divine goddess, I bow to you in reverence.

ଶ୍ରୀ ମହାଲକ୍ଷ୍ମୀଙ୍କର ସଂକ୍ଷିପ୍ତ ପୂଜା

Śrī Mahālakṣmīṅkara Saṅkṣipta Pūjā

Śrī Mahālakṣmīṅkara Saṅkṣipta Pūjā – Concise Worship of Śrī Mahālakṣmī

ଧ୍ୟାନ ମନ୍ତ୍ର

Dhyāna Mantra

Meditation Mantra

ଓଁ ବିଷ୍ଣୁ ଶକ୍ତୌ ଚତୁର୍ଭୁଜା

Oṁ Vishnu śaktau caturbhujā

Om. She who is the power (śakti) of Lord Vishnu, with four arms.

ବୈକୁଣ୍ଠ ବାସିନ୍ୟୈ

Vaikuntha vāsinyaī

Who resides in Vaikuṇṭha (the divine abode of Lord Vishnu).

ଶ୍ରୀ ହ୍ଲୀଂ

Srī h līṁ

"Śrī" (symbol of prosperity) and "Hlīṁ" (a sacred seed syllable associated with Lakṣmī and divine power).

ମହାଲକ୍ଷ୍ମୀ ନାରାୟଣୀ ଦେବ୍ୟୈ

Mahālakṣmī Nārāyaṇī devyai

To the goddess Mahālakṣmī, also known as Nārāyaṇī (consort of Nārāyaṇa / Vishnu).

ନମଃ ।

Namaḥ ll

I offer my salutations / obeisance.

<u>ଗାୟତ୍ରୀ</u>

<u>Gāyatrī</u>

ଓଁ ମହାଲକ୍ଷ୍ମୀ ବିଦ୍ମହେ

Oṁ Mahālakṣmī vidmahe

Om, may we know (meditate upon) Mahālakṣmī.

ବୈକୁଣ୍ଠବାସିନ୍ୟୈ ଧୀମହୀ,

Vaikunthabāsinyai dhīmahi,

Who resides in Vaikuṇṭha (the divine abode of Vishnu), we meditate upon her intellect (divine essence).

ତନ୍ତ୍ରୋ ଲକ୍ଷ୍ମୀ ପ୍ରଚୋଦୟାତ୍ ।

Tantra-Lakṣmī pracodayāt.

May that Lakṣmī, associated with Tantra (spiritual energy), inspire (or awaken) us.

ଧ୍ୟାନ-

Dhyāna

Meditation verse

ଓଁ କାନ୍ତ୍ୟା କାଞ୍ଚନସନ୍ନିଭଂ

Oṁ kāntyā kāñcanasannibhaṁ

Om, (She who is) radiant, resembling pure gold.

ହିମଗିରି ପ୍ରକ୍ଷୈ୍ୟଶ୍ଚ ତୁର୍ଭିର୍ଗଜେଃ ।

Himagiri prakṣyaiś ca turbhir garjeḥ,

Resembling the peaks of the Himalayas and surrounded by (four) elephants.

ହସ୍ତେତ୍ କ୍ଷିପ୍ତ ହିରଣ୍ମୟୀ ମୃତଘଟୈ

Hastet kṣipta hiraṇmayī mṛtaghaṭaiḥ

In Her hands, golden water pots are held or thrown (sprinkled).

ରାଶିଚ୍ୟମାନା ପ୍ରିୟାମ୍,

Rāśi-cyamānāṁ priyām,

Pouring forth abundance, She is beloved.

ବିଭ୍ରାଣଂ ବରମବଜଂ ଯୁଗ୍ମମଭୟଂ

Bibhrāṇaṁ varam-abhayaṁ yugmam abhayaṁ

She holds the boon-giving (vara) and fear-dispelling (abhaya) lotus in her two hands.

ହସ୍ତେ କରୀଟୋଜ୍ୱଳା,

Haste karīṭojjvalāṁ,

Her hands shine with a crown (or bejewelled with a diadem).

କ୍ଷୌମାବଦ୍ଧ ନିତମ୍ବ ବିମଲଲିତଂ

Kṣaumābaddha nitamba vimalalitaṁ

Her waist is adorned with silk, appearing pure and graceful.

ବନ୍ଦେଽରବିନ୍ଦ ସ୍ଥିତଂ ।

Vande'ravinda-sthitām.

I bow to (Her) who is seated on a lotus.

ବୈଦିକ ମନ୍ତ୍ର

Vaidika Mantra

The Vedic Mantra

ଓଁ ଲକ୍ଷ୍ମୀଦେବ୍ୟୈ ନମଃ ।

Oṁ Lakṣmīdevyai namaḥ.

Om, salutations to Goddess Lakshmi.

ଆସନ ମନ୍ତ୍ର

Āsana Mantra

(Offering of highly valuable seat) Mantra

ନାନାରତ୍ନ ସମାଯୁକ୍ତଂ

Nānā-ratna-samāyuktaṁ

Adorned with various gems

କାର୍ତ୍ତିସ୍ୱର ବିଭୂଷିତଂ,

Kārttisvara vibhūṣitaṁ,

Decorated with artistic ornaments

ଆସନଂ ବହୁମୂଲ୍ୟଂ ଚ

Asanaṁ bahumūlyaṁ ca

A seat of great value

ଗୃହିଣ ଜଗଦ୍ଧୀଶ୍ୱରୀ ।

Gṛhiṇa jagadīśvarī ।

Offered to the consort of the Lord of the Universe (Jagadīśvarī – Goddess Lakshmi)

ଇଦଂ ମାନସଂ

Idaṁ mānasaṁ

This (seat) mentally offered (with devotion)

ଓଁ ମହାଲକ୍ଷ୍ମ୍ୟୈ ନମଃ ।

Oṁ Mahālakṣmyai namaḥ.

Salutations to Mahalakshmi

ସ୍ୱାଗତ ମନ୍ତ୍ର

Svāgata Mantra

Welcome Mantra

ସ୍ୱାଗତାର୍ଥଂ ପୁଷ୍ପିପଟକଂ

Svāgatārthaṁ puṣpipatakaṁ

This floral offering (garland or mat of flowers) for the purpose of welcoming

ଗୃହାଣ ବୈକୁଣ୍ଠେଶ୍ୱରୀ ମୟା

Gṛhāṇa Vaikuntheśvarī, maya

Please accept it, O Goddess of Vaikuṇṭha (Lakshmi), offered by me

ନିବେଦିତ ଭକ୍ତ୍ୟା ପ୍ରସନ୍ନାଭବ ସର୍ବଦା ।

Niveditaṁ bhaktyā prasannā bhava sarvadā ǀ

Humbly submitted with devotion; be pleased always

ଭୋ ମାତଃ କମଳା ! ସ୍ୱାଗତଂ ସୁସ୍ୱାଗତଂ ॥

Bho mātaḥ Kamalā! Svāgataṁ su-svāgataṁ ǁ

O Mother Kamala (Lakshmi)! Welcome, welcome indeed!

<u>ଆବାହନ ମନ୍ତ୍ର</u>

<u>Āvāhana Mantra</u>

Invocation Mantra

ଆଗଚ୍ଛ ଦେବ ଦେବେଣି ।

Āgaccha Deva Deveṇi,

Come, O God! O Goddess!

ଦାରିଦ୍ର୍ୟ ଦୁଃଖ ନାଶିନୀ,

Dāridrya-duḥkha-nāśinī,

You who destroy poverty and sorrow

କୃପୟା ଗୃହାଣ ପୂଜାଂ

Kṛpayā gṛhāṇa pūjāṁ mam,

Kindly accept this worship

ମପ୍ରୋତି ପ୍ରସନ୍ନାଭବ ।

Prati prasannā bhava.

Be pleased with me.

ଅର୍ଘ୍ୟ ମନ୍ତ୍ର

Arghya Mantra

Offering Mantra

ଅର୍ଘ୍ୟଂ ଗୃହାଣ ଦେବେଶି ଗନ୍ଧ ପୁଷ୍ପାକ୍ଷତୈର୍ଯୁତଂ,

Arghyaṁ gṛhāṇa deveśi gandha-puṣpākṣataiḥ yutaṁ,

O Goddess, accept this arghya (offering) which is accompanied with fragrance, flowers, and rice grains.

ଅର୍ଷତଂ ତବ ପ୍ରୀତ୍ୟାର୍ଥଂ ପ୍ରସୀଦ ଜଗଦୀଶ୍ୱରୀ ।

Arghyataṁ tava prītyartham prasīda jagadīśvarī I

This is offered for your pleasure. Be gracious, O Goddess of the universe.

ଇଦମର୍ଘ୍ୟ ଓଁ ଶ୍ରୀ ମହାଲକ୍ଷ୍ମୈ୍ୟ ସ୍ୱାହାଃ ॥

Idam arghyaṁ — Oṁ Śrī Mahālakṣmyai svāhā II

This arghya is (offered) to Śrī Mahālakṣmī. Svāhā (may it be accepted).

ପାଦ୍ୟ ମନ୍ତ୍ର

Pādya Mantra

(Washing of Feet) Mantra

ପାଦ୍ୟ ଗୃହାଣ ଦେବେଶି ଶିତଳଂ ସୁମନୋହରଂ,

Pādya gṛhāṇa deveśi śitalaṁ sumanoharaṁ,

O Goddess of the Gods, accept this cool and delightful water for washing the feet.

ଅର୍ପିତ ପରାୟାଭକ୍ତ୍ୟା ଭୁବନାନନ୍ଦ କାରିଣୀ ।

Arpita parāyā bhaktyā bhuvanānanda kāriṇī ।

It is offered with supreme devotion, O one who brings joy to the worlds.

ଏତତ୍ ପାଦ୍ୟଂ ଓଁ ଶ୍ରୀ ମହାଲକ୍ଷ୍ମ୍ୟୈ ନମଃ ॥

Etat pādyaṁ oṁ śrī Mahālakṣmyai namaḥ ।

This is the foot-washing water — obeisance to Śrī Mahālakṣmī.

ସ୍ନାନୀୟ ମନ୍ତ୍ର

Snānīya Mantra

(Bathing Water) Mantra

ନାନା ତୀର୍ଥୋଦ୍ଭବଂବାରୀ ।

Nānā tīrthodbhavaṁ vāri

Water originating from various sacred pilgrimages (holy rivers and places),

କୁଙ୍କୁମାଦୌ ସୁଶିତଳଂ,

Kuṅkumādau suśītalaṁ,

Cool and fragrant with saffron and other sanctifying substances,

ମୟା ସମର୍ପିତଂ ଭକ୍ତ୍ୟା

Mayā samarpitaṁ bhaktyā

Is offered by me with devotion,

ସ୍ନାନାର୍ଥଂ ଲୋକ ଜନନୀ ।

Snānārthaṁ loka-jananī ।

For the purpose of bathing, O Mother of the worlds.

ଇଦଂ ସ୍ନାନୀୟ ଜଳଂ ଓଁ ଶ୍ରୀ ମହାଲକ୍ଷ୍ମ୍ୟୈ-ବଷଟ୍ ।

Idaṁ snānīya-jalaṁ — Oṁ Śrī Mahālakṣmyai vaṣaṭ ॥

This is bathing water — Om, to Śrī Mahālakṣmī, vaṣaṭ (let it be accepted).

ଆଭରଣ ମନ୍ତ୍ର

Ābharaṇa Mantra

(Adornment) Mantra

ନାନା ରତ୍ନ ସମାକୀର୍ଣ୍ଣଂ ମାଳାଂ ସ୍ୱର୍ଣ୍ଣମୟୀ ତଥା,

Nānā-ratna-samākīrṇaṁ mālāṁ svarṇamayī tathā,

A garland adorned with various gems and made of gold as well,

ମୁଦ୍ରିକାଂ ହସ୍ତ ପାଦଞ୍ଚ ଗୃହାଣ ଜଗଦୀଶ୍ୱରୀ,

Mudrikāṁ hasta-pādañ ca gṛhāṇa Jagadīśvarī I

Along with rings for the hands and feet — accept these, O Goddess of the universe,

ଇଦଂ ସ୍ୱର୍ଣ୍ଣମାଳଂ ମୁଦ୍ରିକାଂ ଆଭରଣଂ

Idaṁ svarṇamālāṁ mudrikāṁ ābharaṇaṁ —

This golden garland and rings are ornaments,

ଶ୍ରୀ ମହାଲକ୍ଷ୍ମ୍ୟୈ ନମଃ ।

Śrī Mahālakṣmyai namaḥ II

Salutations to Śrī Mahālakṣmī.

ଆଚମନୀୟ ମନ୍ତ୍ର

Ācamanīya Mantra

(Sipping Water for Purification) Mantra

ନାନା ତୀର୍ଥୋଦ୍ଭବଂ ବାରି କର୍ପୂରାଦୌଃ ସୁବାସିତଂ ।

Nānā tīrthodbhavaṁ vāri karpūra-doḥ subhāsitaṁ I

Water originating from various sacred pilgrimages, fragrant with camphor,

ଗୃହାଣାଚମନୀୟଂ ପ୍ରସନ୍ନାଭବ ଜନନୀ |

Gṛhāṇācamanīyaṁ prasannā bhava Jananī I

Accept this water for sipping (ācamana), O Mother, be pleased,

ଇଦଂ ଆଚମନୀୟ ଓଁ ଶ୍ରୀ ମହାଲକ୍ଷ୍ମୈ୍ୟ ସ୍ୱାହା ।

Idaṁ ācamanīyaṁ — Oṁ Śrī Mahālakṣmyai svāhā II

This is ācamaniya (sipping water) — Oṁ, salutations to Śrī Mahālakṣmī.

ବସନ ମନ୍ତ୍ର

Vasana Mantra

(Offering of Clothes) Mantra

ବିଶୁଦ୍ଧେ ସୌନ୍ଦର୍ଯ୍ୟ କ୍ଷୌମେ ନୂତନ ସୁଶାଟିକେ,

Viśuddhe saundarya-kṣaume nūtana-suśāṭike,

O pure one, in beautiful, elegant, new silken garments,

ମୟା ନିବେଦିତଂ ଭକ୍ତ୍ୟା ଗୃହାଣ ବୈକୁଣ୍ଠେଶ୍ୱରୀ ।

Mayā niveditaṁ bhaktyā gṛhāṇa Vaikuntheśvarī ।

Offered by me with devotion — accept this, O Queen of Vaikuṇṭha (heaven),

ଇଦଂ ସୋଉରୀୟ ଶାଟିକା ବସ୍ତ୍ରଂ ଓଁ ଶ୍ରୀ ମହାଲକ୍ଷ୍ମ୍ୟୈ ସମର୍ପୟାମି ନମଃ ।

Idaṁ saurīya-śāṭikā-vasttraṁ — Oṁ Śrī Mahālakṣmyai samarpyāmi namaḥ ॥

This solar-coloured silk garment — Oṁ, I offer it with reverence to Śrī Mahālakṣmī.

ସୁଗନ୍ଧ ଦ୍ରବ୍ୟ ମନ୍ତ୍ର

Sugandha Dravya Mantra

(Fragrant Substances) Mantra

ଶରୀରନ୍ତେ ନ ଜାନାମି ଚେଷ୍ଟାଂ ଚୈବଚ ଦେବୟୋ ।

Śarīrānte na jānāmi ceṣṭāṁ caiva ca devayoḥ ।

I do not know the proper movements or gestures of the body towards the Deities.

ମୟା ନିବେଦିତାନ୍ ଗନ୍ଧାନ୍ ପ୍ରାଗୃହାଣ ବିଲେପନଃ ।

Mayā niveditān gandhān prāgṛhāṇa bilepanaḥ ॥

Please accept the fragrant substances offered by me as a sacred anointment.

ସିନ୍ଦୁର ମନ୍ତ୍ର

Sindūra Mantra

(Vermilion Offering) Mantra

ଉଦିତାରୁଣ ସଂକାଶଂ

Uditāruṇa-saṅkāśaṁ

Of the colour like the rising reddish sun

ଜବା କୁସୁମ ସନ୍ନାଭଂ ।

Javā-kusuma-sannibham I

Resembling the hibiscus flower

ସୀମନ୍ତ ଭୂଷଣାର୍ଥାୟ

Sīmantabhūṣaṇārthāya

For the purpose of adorning the parting of the hair (sīmanta)

ସିନ୍ଦୂରଂପ୍ରତି ଗୃହ୍ୟତାଂ ।

Sindūraṁ prati gṛhyatām II

May this sindura (vermilion) be accepted

** କଜ୍ଜଳଂ ମନ୍ତ୍ର**

Kajjala Mantra

(Kohl Application) Mantra

କଜ୍ଜଳଂ କାମିକଂ ରମ୍ୟଂ

Kajjalaṁ kāmikaṁ ramyaṁ

The collyrium (kajal) which is desirable and lovely

କାମିନୀ କାମ ସମ୍ଭବଂ ।

Kāminī kāma-saṁbhavam I

Born of desire and pleasing to a beloved woman

ନେତ୍ରୟୋ ରଞ୍ଜନାର୍ଥାୟ

Netrayoḥ rañjanārthāya

For the purpose of beautifying the two eyes

କଜ୍ଜଳଂ ପ୍ରତି ଗୃହ୍ୟତାଂ ॥

Kajjalaṁ prati gṛhyatām II

May this kajal be accepted

ଅଲତା ମନ୍ତ୍ର

Alatā Mantra

(Red Dye for Feet) Mantra

ବନ୍ଧୁକ କୁସୁମଭାଷା

Bandhūka-kusuma-bhāsā

Of the colour of the bandhūka flower (hibiscus)

ବାଲାର୍କଦ୍ୟୁତି ଗଞ୍ଜନଂ

Bālārka-dyuti-gañjanam I

Resembling the radiance of the rising sun

ପାଦ ଶୋଭା ମୟହଂ ଦେବୀ !

Pāda-śobhā-mayaṁ Devī!

O Goddess! That which enhances the beauty of the feet

ଗୃହୀତାଂ ଜଗଦ୍ଧୀଶ୍ୱରୀ II

Gṛhītam Jagadīśvarī II

May it be accepted, O Goddess of the universe

ପାଦୁକା ମନ୍ତ୍ର

Pādukā Mantra

(Footwear Offering) Mantra

ପାପମଗଘ୍ନନ୍ତି

Pāpam aghayanti

That which removes (destroys) sins

ଗ୍ରୀଷ୍ମ ବର୍ଷା ନିବାରଣାର୍ଥକଂ,

Grīṣma-varṣā-nivāraṇārthakam,

And serves the purpose of protection from summer and rain

ନିବେଦିତଂ ମୟାଦେବୀ ।

Niveditaṁ mayā Devī

Offered by me, O Goddess

ପାଦୁକାଂ ପ୍ରତି ଗୃହ୍ୟତାଂ ।

Pādukāṁ prati gṛhyatām ll

May this pair of sandals (footwear) be accepted

ଚନ୍ଦନ ମନ୍ତ୍ର

Candana Mantra

(Sandalwood Paste) Mantra

ଚନ୍ଦନଂ ଶୀତଳଂ ରମ୍ୟ

Candanaṁ śītalaṁ ramyaṁ

Sandalwood (paste), cool and pleasant

ସୌରଭଂ ଦେବତା ପ୍ରିୟଂ

Saurabhaṁ Devatā-priyam,

Fragrant and dear to the deities

ଶ୍ରଦ୍ଧୟା ଚାର୍ପିତଂ ଦେବୀଂ ।

Sraddhayā cārpitaṁ Devīṁ

Offered with devotion to the Goddess

ଗୃହ୍ୟତାଂ ଧନଦେ ଶୁଭେ ।

Gṛhyatāṁ Dhanade śubhe ।

May it be accepted, O auspicious giver of wealth

ଏଷଃ ଗନ୍ଧଃ

Eṣaḥ gandhaḥ

This is the fragrance (sandalwood paste)

ଓଁ ମହାଲକ୍ଷ୍ମୈ ନମଃ ।

Oṁ Mahālakṣmyai namaḥ ॥

Om, salutations to Mahalakshmi

ପୁଷ୍ପଦାନ ମନ୍ତ୍ର

Puṣpadāna Mantra

(Offering of Flowers) Mantra

ନାନା ବିଧାନ ପୁଷ୍ପାଣି

Nānā-vidhāna puṣpāṇi

Various kinds of flowers

ନାନାଗନ୍ଧ ଯୁତାନ ଚ

Nānā-gandha-yutāna ca,

Accompanied with various fragrances

ନାନା ବର୍ଣ୍ଣାନ୍ୟା ହୃତାନି

Nānā varṇānyā htatāni

Of various colours, offered (by me)

ଶୋଭାର୍ଥଂ ପ୍ରତି ଗୃହ୍ୟତାଂ,

Sobhārthaṁ prati gṛhyatāṁ ।

For the sake of beauty, may they be accepted

ଇଦଂ ପୁଷ୍ପଂ

Idaṁ puṣpaṁ

This flower

ଓଁ ଶ୍ରୀ ମହାଲକ୍ଷ୍ମୈ ବଷଟ୍ ।

Oṁ Śrī Mahālakṣmyai vaṣaṭ ll

Om, to Sri Mahalakshmi, vaṣaṭ (sacrificial offering exclamation)

ଧୂପ ନିବେଦନ ମନ୍ତ୍ର

Dhūpa Nivedana Mantra

(Offering of Incense) Mantra

ବନସ୍ପତି ରସୋଦ୍ଭୂତୋ।

Vanaspati rase.bhūte

Produced from the essence (sap) of forest trees

ଗନ୍ଧାଢ୍ୟୋ।।

Gandha.ḍhye

Rich in fragrance

ସୁମନୋହରଃ ।

Sumanoharaḥ.

Very pleasing to the mind

ଆଘ୍ରେୟ ସର୍ବ ଦେବାନାଂ

Aaghreya sarva Devānāṁ

Meant to be inhaled by all the Gods

ଧୂପୋୟଂ ପ୍ରତି ଗୃହ୍ୟତାଂ

Dhūpoyaṁ prati gṛhyatāṁ

This incense, may it be accepted

ଏଷଃ ଧୂପଃ

Eṣaḥ dhūpaḥ

This is the incense

ଓଁ ଶ୍ରୀ ମହାଲକ୍ଷ୍ମୈ ସ୍ୱାହା ।

Oṁ śrī Mahālakṣmyai svāhā.

Om, to Sri Mahalakshmi, svāhā (offering invocation)

ଦୀପଦାନ ମନ୍ତ୍ର

Dīpadāna Mantra

(Offering of the Lamp) Mantra

ସ୍ୱପ୍ରକାଶ୍ୟ

Svaprakaśya

Self-luminous

ମହାଜ୍ୟୋତି

Mahajyoti

Great light

ସ୍ତିମିରୀ ପତ୍ନଃ

Stimīrī patnaḥ

Remover of darkness

ସଦାହ୍ୟାଭ୍ୟନ୍ତର ଜ୍ୟୋତି

Sadāhyabhyantara jyotir

Always shining as the inner light within the heart

ଦୀପେୟଂ ପ୍ରତି ଗୃହ୍ୟତାଂ । ନୈବେଦ୍ୟ

Dīpeyaṁ prati gṛhyatāṁ naivedya

May this lamp be accepted (as an offering)

ନିବେଦନ ମନ୍ତ୍ର

Nivedana Mantra

(Offering of Food) Mantra

ଶର୍କରା ଖଣ୍ଡ ସଂଯୁକ୍ତଂ

Sarkarā khaṇḍa saṁyuktaṁ

Mixed with pieces of sugar (rock sugar/crystals of sugar)

ଦଧିଦୁଗ୍ଧ ଘୃତାନ୍ୱିତଂ ।

Dadhidugdha ghṛtānvitaṁ |

Accompanied with yogurt, milk, and ghee

ଲେହ୍ୟପେୟଂ ଭକ୍ଷଭେଜ୍ୟଂ

Lehyapeyaṁ bhakṣabhejyam

Lickables, drinkables, eatables, and solid foods

ନୈବେଦ୍ୟ ପ୍ରତି ଗୃହ୍ୟତାଂ ।

Naivedya prati gṛhyatāṁ.

May this offering of food be accepted

ଏଷନୈବେଦ୍ୟଂ ଓଁ ଶ୍ରୀ ମହାଲକ୍ଷ୍ମୈ୍ୟ ସ୍ୱାହା ।

Eṣanaivedyaṁ oṁ śrī Mahālakṣmyai svāhā.

This is the offering — Om, to Mahalakshmi, I make this offering.

ତାମ୍ବୁଲ ମନ୍ତ୍ର

Tāmbūla Mantra

(Offering of Betel Leaves) Mantra

ପୁଗିଫଳା ଲବଙ୍ଗଞ୍ଚ

Pugiphalā lavaṅgañca

Areca nut (betel nut) and clove

ପକ୍ୱ ପର୍ଣ୍ଣ ଦଳୈର୍ୟତଂ

Pakva parṇṇa daḷairyataṁ

Combined with ripe betel leaves

କର୍ପୁରୈକୀ ସମାୟୁତଂ

Karpuraikī samāyutaṁ

Mixed with camphor and other fragrant substances

ତାମ୍ବୁଳଂ ପ୍ରତି ଗୃହ୍ୟତାଂ ।

Tāmbuḷaṁ prati gṛhyatāṁ.

May this betel offering be accepted

ଏସ ତାମ୍ବୁଳଂ ଓଁ ଶ୍ରୀ ମହାଲକ୍ଷ୍ମୈ୍ୟ ସ୍ୱାହା ।

Esa tāmbuḷaṁ oṁ śrī Mahālakṣmyai svāhā.

This is the betel offering. Om, to Mahalakshmi, Svaha (I reverently offer it).

ପୁଷ୍ପାଞ୍ଜଳି ମନ୍ତ୍ର

Puṣpāñjali Mantra

(Offering of Flower Handful) Mantra

ନମଃ ଦେବୀ ମହାଲକ୍ଷ୍ମୀ

Namaḥ Devī Mahālakṣmī

Salutations to the Goddess Mahalakshmi

ସର୍ବ ସମ୍ପଦ ଦାୟିନୀ

Sarva sampada dāyinī

Giver of all wealth and prosperity

ସର୍ବ ଦୁଃଖ ହାରିଃଦେବୀ

Sarva duḥkha hāriḥ Devī

O Goddess, remover of all sorrow

ଗୃହାଣ କୁସୁମାଞ୍ଜଳିଂ ।

Gṛhāṇa kusumāñjaliṁ.

Please accept this offering of flowers (handful of flowers)

ସ୍ତୁତିପାଠ ମନ୍ତ୍ର

Stutipāṭha Mantra

(Hymn of Praise) Mantra

ନମସ୍ତେଷୁ ମହାମାୟେ

Namasteṣu Mahāmāye

Salutations to you, O great enchantress (Mahāmāyā)

ଶ୍ରୀପୀଠେ ସୁରପୂଜିତେ ।

Srīpīṭhe surapūjite |

Who resides in the seat of prosperity (śrīpīṭha) and is worshipped by the Gods (sura-pūjite)

ଶଙ୍ଖ ଚକ୍ର ଗଦାହସ୍ତେ

Saṅkha cakra gadāhaste

Who holds a conch (śaṅkha), discus (cakra), and mace (gadā) in Her hands

ମହାଲକ୍ଷ୍ମୀ ନମୋଃସ୍ତୁତେ ।

Mahālakṣmī namo'stute |

O Mahalakshmi, I bow to you

କ୍ଷମାପ୍ରାର୍ଥନା ମନ୍ତ୍ର

Kṣamāprārthanā Mantra

(Apology Prayer) Mantra

ମନ୍ତ୍ର ତନ୍ତ୍ର କ୍ରିୟାଚାର ଭାବ ଭକ୍ତ୍ୟା ନ୍ୟଥାକୃତମ୍ ।

Mantra tantra kriyācāra bhāva bhaktyā nyathākṛtam |

Whatever has been done incorrectly in mantra, tantra, ritual actions, conduct, feeling, or devotion

ଯଦଚ୍ଛିର୍ତତଂ ମହାଦେବୀ,

Yadacchirtataṁ Mahādevī,

Whatever was omitted, O Great Goddess (Mahādevī)

ପରିପୂର୍ଣ୍ଣଂତଦସ୍ତୁମେ ।

Paripūrṇantadastume |

May that (all) be considered complete (fulfilled) for me

ପ୍ରଣାମ ମନ୍ତ୍ର

Praṇāma Mantra

Salutation Mantra

ବିଶ୍ୱ ରୂପସ୍ୟ ଭାର୍ଯ୍ୟାସି ପଦ୍ମେ ପଦ୍ମାଳୟେ ଶୁଭେ

Biśva rūpasya bhāryāsi padme padmālaye śubhe

O Auspicious One, O Padmā (Goddess Lakshmi), who resides in the lotus and is the consort of the one who embodies the form of the universe (Viṣhṇu)

ସର୍ବ୍ଦତଃ ପାହିମାଂ ଦେବୀ ମହାଲକ୍ଷ୍ମୀ ନମୋଽସ୍ତୁତେ ।

Sarddhataḥ pāhimāṁ Devī Mahālakṣmī namo'stute.

Protect me completely, O Goddess Mahālakṣmī, salutations to You

ବନ୍ଦେହଂ ଧନଦାତ୍ରୀ ମହାଲକ୍ଷ୍ମୀଂ ଦେବୀ ନମୋନମାମି ।

Bandehaṁ dhanadātrī Mahālakṣmīṁ Devī namonamāmi.

I bow down to Mahālakṣmī, the giver of wealth — salutation after salutation to the Goddess

ମାତା ଲକ୍ଷ୍ମୀଙ୍କୁ ପଦ୍ମଫୁଲ ଦେଇ ପୂଜା କଲେ ପୂଜାର ସୁଫଳ ମିଳେ ଓ ମହାଲକ୍ଷ୍ମୀ ସନ୍ତୁଷ୍ଟ ହୋଇଥାଆନ୍ତି।

Mātā Lakṣmīṁku padma-phula dei pūjā kale pūjāra suphala miḷe o Mahālakṣmī santuṣṭa hoithāanti I

If one worships Mother Lakshmi by offering lotus flowers, one receives the fruitful result of that worship, and Mahālakṣmī becomes pleased.

ଇତି ଶ୍ରୀ ଲକ୍ଷ୍ମୀ ପୁରାଣ ସମ୍ପୂର୍ଣ୍ଣ

Iti Śrī Lakṣmī Purāṇa sampūrṇa.

Thus ends the Śrī Lakṣmī Purāṇa in its entirety.

May Her light lead you to prosperity and peace.

Om Lakşmyai Namah

www.ingramcontent.com/pod-product-compliance
Lightning Source LLC
Chambersburg PA
CBHW062104160726
48282CB00026B/660

* 9 7 8 9 3 3 4 3 6 5 3 6 8 *